Since
1·7·7·6

Since 1·7·7·6

A
Year-By-Year Timeline
of American History

by Paul C. Murphy

PRICE STERN SLOAN

Published by Price Stern Sloan, Inc.
360 N. La Cienega Boulevard
Los Angeles, California 90048

ISBN: 0-8431-2276-5

Introduction

SINCE 1776 is the all-new, revised and updated year-by-year timeline of American history. Here is a key to unlock the door of our nation's past. Learning about the past can be a great adventure and this handy book is a perfect place to start. All entries are made in clear, concise language to give you the fast facts you need to know.

Of course, what you will find here is a brief, and by no means complete, look at American history, but it will surely leave you eager to explore these events further on your own.

Welcome to your heritage!

1776

politics

Thomas Jefferson advanced a plan for resettlement of Negro slaves in Africa.

Thomas Paine first demanded complete independence for the Colonies.

North Carolina became the first colony to formally propose independence.

Thomas Paine wrote his pamphlet "The Crisis," which contained the famous words, "These are the times that try men's souls."

Norfolk, VA was burned by the British.

Charleston, SC set up an independent government.

Nathan Hale, hanged in New York, spoke the famed words, "I only regret that I have but one life to lose for my country."

The Declaration of Independence was drafted by Thomas Jefferson.

New Jersey became the first colony to grant women suffrage (voting rights). The decision was later reversed.

Congress resolved to call the new country "the United States," replacing the old title of United Colonies.

American forces were defeated at Long Island and Fort Washington, NY.

General Washington captured 1,000 Hessian troops at Trenton, NJ.

Esek Hopkins was named first commander in chief of the Continental Navy.

Congress elected Ben Franklin to represent the U.S. in establishing a commerce treaty with France.

"E Pluribus Unum" was suggested as the motto for the U.S. seal.

General Washington crossed the Delaware River.

Patrick Henry became the governor of Virginia.

The first American war submarine was constructed. *The Turtle* held a crew of one.

James Monroe graduated from William & Mary College in Virginia.

religion

The presidio of San Francisco, CA was founded and established as a mission.

The mission of San Juan Capistrano was established in California.

arts & culture

The first cocktails were made by a barmaid in Elmsford, NY who garnished them with feathers.

Phi Beta Kappa became the first social fraternity in America. It later became an honorary fraternity.

1777

politics

General Washington defeated the British army at the battle of Princeton, NJ but was repulsed at Germantown, PA.

Count Pulaski was commissioned as a brigadier general.

American troops twice thwarted British General John Burgoyne in his attempts to open a military route from Bemis Heights to Albany, NY in the Freeman's Farm Battles.

American troops were repulsed at Monmouth, NJ.

Vermont declared itself an independent state.

Fort Ticonderoga, NY was abandoned by the Americans.

The pueblo of San Jose, CA was established.

Under Cornwallis, British troops took possession of Philadelphia, PA.

The Continental Congress adopted the flag of thirteen stars and stripes.

The state of Vermont abolished slavery.

Henry Clay was born in Kentucky.

The Articles of Confederation were adopted by the Continental Congress at York, PA.

British supply ships were sunk near Amboy.

French general Lafayette volunteered his services to Congress and met with General Washington.

Major battles were fought at Oriskany, NY and Hubbardton and Bennington, VT.

The new stars and stripes flag was first officially carried into battle at the Battle of Brandywine.

David Bushnell, inventor of the man-powered submarine, laid the first-known marine mine field against the British.

John Adams was named U.S. commissioner to France (1777-1779).

In his ship the *Ranger*, Captain John Paul Jones took several British ships.

General Washington established winter headquarters at Valley Forge, PA.

The *Raleigh* became the first ship to fly the American flag on high seas.

America received its first loan for war purposes from France.

Monterey, CA was established as the capital of Spanish California.

science & technology

J. Wilkinson of Rhode Island invented the process of cutting nails from cold iron.

arts & culture

The first English Bible was published in America (New Testament only).

The Seasons by James Thomson were among the most popular poems of the day.

1778

politics

The Continental Congress ratified a treaty of alliance with France.

Baron Steuben joined the camp at Valley Forge.

Americans broke camp at Valley Forge and pursued the British.

The U.S. Secret Service was organized by Aaron Burr, who became its first director.

The British evacuated Philadelphia and retreated to New Jersey.

American forces evacuated Rhode Island.

British troops took Savannah, GA.

The oath of office for the U.S. Army was prescribed by Congress.

England appointed peace commissioners to America.

The French fleet, under Count D'Estaing, arrived at Narragansett Bay.

The British bill by Lord North seeking peace negotiations was rejected by Congress.

The Wyoming Valley Massacre, in which a small American settlement in northeastern PA was overwhelmed by combined British and Indian forces, occurred.

Ben Franklin was appointed U.S. minister to France.

The first arsenal was established at Springfield, MA.

General Lincoln and the American Army surrendered at Charleston, SC.

Major battles were fought at Little Egg Harbor and Chestnut Neck, NJ.

Daniel Boone and twenty-seven men were captured by Indians at Blue Lick, KY.

Mohawk Indians plundered and burned Cobleskill, NY.

The British fleet, bringing Clinton's army, arrived off Newport.

General Washington met with Congress in Philadelphia.

The first treaty was established between the U.S. and Indian tribes.

General Washington established winter headquarters at Middlebrook, NJ.

1779

politics

John Paul Jones made his historic statement, "I have not yet begun to fight."

The first salute to the U.S. flag was fired by a French ship.

Americans won a victory at Kettle Creek, GA.

Count Pulaski, the famous Polish officer in the American service, was mortally wounded in battle.

Congress called upon states for quotas of $15 million for the year and $6 million annually thereafter for eighteen years for a sinking fund.

British troops under General McLane took possession of Castine, ME.

American troops under Major Clark captured Vincennes, IN.

Spain declared war against England.

Fort Stony Point on the Hudson River was captured by the British.

Americans were repulsed at Stone Ferry, SC.

British troops plundered and burned New Haven, Fairfield, and Norwalk, CT.

Rhode Island was evacuated by British troops.

Thomas Jefferson became governor of Virginia.

The U.S. concluded an alliance with Spain.

John Rutledge was elected governor of South Carolina.

The colony of Georgia was held by the British.

A battle was fought at Powlee Hook, NJ.

Captain Cook was killed at Kealakekua Bay, HI.

Ships carrying 8,000 British troops sailed from New York to Charleston, SC.

James Robertson and 300 followers descended the Cumberland River valley and founded Nashville, TN.

Lexington, KY was permanently settled and a fort was established there.

The first military drill manual was published in Philadelphia.

U.S. Army uniforms were standardized.

The U.S. Army Corps of Engineers was established.

The American Army wintered at Morristown, NJ.

science & technology

At this time the oyster industry was flourishing in Rhode Island.

arts & culture

America's first law school to be affiliated with a college was established in Williamsburg, VA.

The University of Pennsylvania became the first college legally designated as a university.

1780

politics

British and Tory troops were defeated at King's Mountain, SC.

Henry Laurens, former president of the Second Continental Congress, was captured by the British while on his way to negotiate a treaty between the U.S. and Holland.

The state of Pennsylvania abolished slavery.

Mobile, AL was captured by the Spanish under DeGalvez, the governor of Louisiana.

Charleston, SC surrendered to the British.

Pembina, ND was settled by the French.

British troops seized distinguished citizens of Carolina and transported them to Augustine, FL.

John Hancock became governor of Massachusetts.

James Madison became a delegate to Congress from Virginia (1780-1783).

Benedict Arnold deserted to the British ship *Vulture*.

At the Battle of Camden, 2,000 American troops were killed, wounded or captured.

British troops crossed to Staten Island in the Battle of Springfield, NJ.

Louisville, KY was incorporated as a town.

Russia proclaimed its armed neutrality in the war.

The Spanish fleet appeared off Pensacola, FL, but did not attack.

General Lafayette landed in Boston and proceeded to Morristown.

Johnstown, NY was burned by Tories and Indians.

The French fleet arrived at Newport with 6,000 French soldiers.

American troops were repulsed by the British at Augusta, GA.

American Major Andre was hanged at Tappan, NY for treason.

Benedict Arnold embarked for Virginia with the British.

General Washington established winter headquarters at New Windsor, NY.

science & technology

The first hat factory in America was established at Danbury, CT.

arts & culture

The estimated colonial population at this time was 2,781,000.

The first town clock in the country was mounted in New York City.

The American Academy of Arts and Sciences was chartered in Boston, MA.

The Humane Society of Philadelphia organized the First Aid Emergency Organization.

1781

politics

religion

The French fleet engaged the British fleet in Chesapeake Bay.

Benedict Arnold and British troops plundered and burned Richmond, VA.

Allied armies marched across New Jersey en route to Yorktown, VA.

American and French forces left the Hudson River to capture Cornwallis.

Andrew Jackson was wounded by a British officer.

Benjamin Lincoln was appointed secretary of war by Congress.

U.S. troops defeated the British at Cowpens and Eutaw Springs, SC.

New London, CT was seized and burned by British General Benedict Arnold.

Cornwallis surrendered 7,000 troops to Generals Washington and Lafayette at Yorktown, VA.

The American Revolution ended in victory for the United States.

A day of thanksgiving was observed throughout the U.S.

Settlers on the Cumberland River in Tennessee repulsed attacks by Indians.

The Spanish captured the British fort at St. Joseph in Michigan.

The Vermont Legislature applied for entry into the Union as a state.

Pensacola and West Florida surrendered to Spanish Governor DeGalvez.

At the end of the American Revolution, General Washington commanded 17,300 troops. Massachusetts and Connecticut had furnished more troops than any other states.

America's first government incorporated bank was chartered in Philadelphia by Congress.

Franciscan monks settled in Los Angeles.

1782

politics

The Great Seal of the United States, with the motto "E Pluribus Unum," was adopted.

The giving of the Purple Heart medal to those wounded in battle was initiated by George Washington.

Martin Van Buren was born in Kinderhook, NY.

Holland recognized the independence of the United States.

Americans battled Indians at Sandusky, OH.

The U.S. and France agreed upon a repayment plan at Versailles for the war loan.

The U.S. and England signed preliminary articles of peace in Paris.

The French army embarked from Boston.

James Monroe became a member of the Virginia Assembly.

Washington urged state governors to pay sums to support Congress.

Vermont accepted conditions of admission to the Union.

The presidio and military town of Santa Barbara, CA was founded.

The British House of Commons resolved against further war in North America.

The British Parliament acted to enable the king to make peace with America.

Sir Guy Carleton was sent from England to America to carry out peace conditions.

John Jay and John Adams joined Ben Franklin in Paris to negotiate peace.

Thomas Jefferson estimated the cost of the war at $140 million.

The entire foreign debt at this time was $7,885,085.

arts & culture

The first Bible was printed in the United States in Philadelphia.

The song "Yankee Doodle" first appeared in print.

Samuel Stearns published the first nautical almanac in America.

The Harvard Medical School opened.

Washington College in Maryland was the first to be named in George Washington's honor.

1783

politics

*science &
technology*

The Continental Congress met in Annapolis, MD.

Peace was proclaimed by Congress.

The Continental Congress was renamed the Congress of the Confederation.

Congress ordered the army disbanded, with a small force to remain in West Point, NY.

Charleston, SC and Savannah, GA were evacuated by the British.

General Washington resigned his commission as commander in chief of the U.S. Army at Annapolis, MD.

British forces evacuated New York City, the last post held by England in the U.S.

The treaty officially ending the Revolutionary War was signed with Great Britain. The treaty had been negotiated by John Adams.

Soldiers rioted in Philadelphia to demand back pay.

The U.S. contracted with France for a new loan.

Washington received an official expression of gratitude from Congress at Nassau Hall, NJ.

Slave trading was outlawed in Maryland.

Thomas Jefferson and James Monroe were elected members of Congress from Virginia.

George Washington returned to his Mount Vernon estate.

War veterans organized the Society of the Cincinnati.

Slavery was made illegal in Massachusetts.

Sweden, Denmark and Russia recognized U.S. independence.

Florida was returned to Spain by the British, in exchange for the Bahamas. Over 10,000 people fled Florida.

The estimated contributions of the states of the Continental Army during the war totaled $231,771.

The public debt at this time was estimated at $42 million.

Benjamin Franklin invented bifocal spectacles.

1784

politics

The Treaty of Paris between the U.S. and England was ratified by Congress.

Zachary Taylor was born in Orange Court House, VA.

New Haven, CT, Newport, RI and Nashville, TN were established.

Spain took possession of St. Augustine, FL.

Congress convened in Trenton, NJ.

Patrick Henry became governor of Virginia.

Franklin, an area in western North Carolina, was organized as a state but never recognized.

The first major depression occurred in the U.S. (1784-1789).

George Washington helped to form the Potomac Land Company.

The *Empress of China* became the first American ship to enter the port of Canton, China.

An American ship on the Mississippi River was seized by the Spanish at Natchez, MS.

Spain informed the U.S. that American ships on the Mississippi River in Spanish territory would be seized.

James Madison was elected to the Virginia Legislature (1784-1786).

The first Russian settlement was established in Alaska, on Kodiak Island in Three Saints Bay.

North Carolina offered to cede all of its western lands to the federal government.

science & technology

James Rumsey invented and demonstrated the first motorboat.

The first seed business in the U.S. was founded in Philadelphia.

religion

The Methodist Church was organized in America in Baltimore, MD.

The first theological school in the U.S. was established in New York City.

arts & culture

The first daily newspaper in America, the *American Daily Advertiser*, was published in Philadelphia.

Edward Warren made the first balloon flight in Baltimore, MD.

Jedidiah Morse published the first geography book in New Haven, CT.

The first law school in the U.S. was established at Litchfield, CT.

1785

politics

Slavery was made illegal in New York.

Thomas Jefferson proposed a coinage system to Congress.

The state of Virginia authorized the first American turnpike.

John Adams became the first U.S. envoy to England.

Congress met in New York, NY.

Congress adopted the decimal system for money, with the dollar as the unit.

Franklin and Adams concluded a treaty of amity and commerce with Prussia.

The Arkansas Territory was first settled at Arkansas Post.

Thomas Jefferson succeeded Ben Franklin as minister to France.

Ben Franklin became the president of Pennsylvania.

Congress first provided for carrying mail by stagecoach.

George Washington selected the site for a permanent capital of the U.S.

General Henry Knox was appointed secretary of war.

The U.S. Army was organized with 700 men enlisted for three years.

The U.S. concluded a treaty with the Cherokee Indians.

The separation of the district of Maine from Massachusetts was considered.

science & technology

The first marble quarry was established in Dorset, VT.

religion

The first Unitarian Church, Episcopalian King's Chapel, was established in the U.S. in Boston.

The first annual conference of the Methodist Church in America was held in Louisburg, NC.

arts & culture

Dr. Benjamin Rush set up the first dispensary in America in Philadelphia.

Macpherson's Directory, the first city directory in the U.S., was published in Philadelphia.

The University of Georgia was chartered, making it the oldest state university in America.

The first farmers' cooperative groups in America were formed in Pennsylvania and South Carolina.

The term "face the music" entered theater jargon about this time. It referred to the actor facing the footlights.

1786

politics

Slavery was outlawed in New Jersey.

New Jersey refused to pay its quota to Congress.

David Crockett was born in Hawkins County, TN.

James Madison was appointed to the Virginia Legislature.

Congress passed an ordinance establishing the U.S. Mint.

A convention was held in Annapolis to consider changes in the Articles of Confederation.

A bill for establishing religious freedom was enacted by the state of Virginia.

Shay's Rebellion, the first against the federal government, took place in Massachusetts. Shay, a former army officer, led the revolt against taxes, and lawyers' fees and practices.

Cleveland, OH was established as a trading post.

The Pribilof Islands were discovered in the Pacific Ocean.

The U.S. signed a treaty with the Choctaw, Chickasaw and Shawnee Indians.

Over a million acres of land owned by Massachusetts were disposed of by lottery.

The boundary dispute between New York and Massachusetts was settled.

Congress demanded that Spain grant the U.S. shipping rights on the Mississippi River.

Armed mobs in New Hampshire threatened the state legislature, demanding paper money and distribution of property.

science & technology

The first steamboat in America was built on the Delaware River.

Daniel Jackson operated the first cotton-spinning jenny at Providence, RI.

religion

The Santa Barbara, CA mission was founded by the Spanish.

The first known Sunday school in America was established in Hanover County, VA.

arts & culture

The first U.S. performance of *Hamlet* opened in New York City.

The first musical periodical in America was published in Connecticut.

Printers in Philadelphia staged the first recorded strike in the U.S.

The first country club in America was formed in Charleston, SC.

1787

politics

The Constitutional Convention met in Philadelphia.

George Washington was elected president of the Constitutional Convention.

The Small State Plan of the Federal Constitution, by William Patterson of New Jersey, was presented to the Constitutional Convention.

Delegates to the Convention signed the Constitution, as amended, and adjourned.

A draft of the Constitution was presented to Congress with a letter from George Washington.

Delaware became the first state to ratify the Constitution, followed by Pennsylvania and New Jersey.

With the signing and ratification of the Constitution, the United States government was formed.

Congress provided a mode of government for the Northwest Territory (now Ohio, Indiana, Illinois, Michigan and Wisconsin) with the Northwest Ordinance.

Captain John Paul Jones's naval achievements in the War of Independence earned him a Congressional gold medal and the title "Father of the U.S. Navy."

James Monroe began a law practice in Fredericksburg, VA.

Shay's Rebellion was completely defeated.

The "Fugio" one cent coin was issued by the U.S. government.

The boundary between Georgia and South Carolina was established at the Tugaloo River.

The *Columbia*, the first ship to carry the U.S. flag around the world, left Boston.

science & technology

Oliver Evans applied for a patent on his steam-propelled vehicles (early automobiles).

The first window glass factory was chartered in Boston.

Levi Hutchins of Concord, NH constructed the first alarm clock.

religion

The first community of Shakers was formed at Mt. Lebanon, NY.

arts & culture

One of the earliest books of secular music was published in New Haven, CT.

1788

politics

The last Congress of the Confederation met in New York. Afterward, it became the U.S. Congress.

After Congress adjourned on November 1, there was no national government until April, 1789.

John Quincy Adams graduated from Harvard.

Georgia, Connecticut, Massachusetts, Maryland, South Carolina, New Hampshire and New York ratified the Constitution.

Rhode Island submitted ratification of the Constitution to the people for a vote.

The District of Columbia, Washington City was established under the Constitution.

Cincinnati, OH was established as Losantiville.

Andrew Jackson moved to Nashville, TN and began a law practice.

A devastating fire destroyed 800 buildings in New Orleans.

The state of Franklin (Frankland) ended with the term of its first governor, John Sevier. Sevier was arrested in North Carolina for high treason and later released.

Slave trading was prohibited in Massachusetts.

The crime of murder was made punishable by death in what is now Ohio.

New York City was declared the temporary capital of the U.S.

A Spanish plot to separate Kentucky from the Union was fostered by J. Wilkinson.

The first national election was authorized by Congress.

science & technology

John Fitch launched the third steamboat in the Delaware River.

The practice of surgical dissection provoked serious rioting in New York City.

The first wool mill powered by water was founded in Hartford, CT.

The *Northwest America* was the first ship to be built on the Pacific Coast.

The first cotton mill was established in Beverly, MA.

The first sailcloth factory was established in Boston, MA.

arts & culture

The first American edition of *The Royal Standard English Dictionary* was published.

Cotton was first planted in Georgia.

The first trotting horses were imported to the U.S.

1789

politics

George Washington was inaugurated as the first president of the U.S. John Adams was his vice president.

The first session of the U.S. Congress was held in New York City.

North Carolina became the twelfth state to ratify the Constitution.

Congress created the U.S. State Department.

The U.S. War Department was created with Henry Knox as its first secretary. The Army at this time had 840 men.

The U.S. Treasury Department was created. Alexander Hamilton became the first U.S. treasurer.

John Jay became the first chief justice of the U.S. Supreme Court.

The District of Columbia was ceded to the U.S. by Maryland and Virginia.

Congress became entangled in a long dispute over Washington's title.

James Madison sponsored the Bill of Rights (the first ten amendments to the Constitution) in Congress.

The U.S. Supreme Court was established by the Judiciary Act.

New Jersey was the first state to ratify the Bill of Rights.

The Office of Postmaster General was created under the Treasury Department.

Congress established the salaries of the president ($25,000), vice president ($5,000), secretary of state ($3,500), secretary of the treasury ($3,500), and secretary of war ($3,000). Congressmen received $6 for each day in session plus mileage.

religion

The Church of England in the U.S. was reorganized as the Episcopal Church.

arts & culture

Thanksgiving Day was celebrated as a national holiday.

The first organized temperance group in the U.S. was formed in Connecticut.

The first bourbon whiskey was distilled by the Reverend Elijah Craig in Bourbon County, KY.

The first road map in the U.S. was published in New York City.

1790

politics

Congress met in New York to hear President Washington give his first annual address.

Rhode Island ratified the Constitution.

Congress authorized the first census. The population of the Union was placed at 3,929,625.

Thomas Jefferson became the first secretary of state.

Benjamin Franklin died in Philadelphia at the age of 84. French National Assembly members wore mourning clothes for Franklin for three days.

The U.S. system of finance was adopted.

The first U.S. copyright act was signed by President Washington.

The U.S. Patent Office opened.

Congress authorized interest-bearing government bonds.

The Federal Naturalization Act was passed by Congress.

John Tyler was born in Greenway, VA.

The seat of national government was moved from New York to Philadelphia.

William Henry Harrison graduated from college.

The Revenue Cutter Service (later the U.S. Coast Guard) was established.

A war with the Northwest Indians began (1790-1795).

science & technology

The first U.S. patent was granted to S. Hopkins to manufacture glass.

Duncan Phyfe, a Scottish immigrant, opened a chair shop in New York.

The first U.S. manufacturer of wooden clocks opened in Waterbury, CT.

S. Slater opened the first cotton carding and spindle mill in Rhode Island.

The first dental drill was invented by John Greenwood.

religion

John Carroll became the first Catholic bishop in the U.S.

The first Catholic Bible was printed in America.

arts & culture

Philadelphia was the largest city in the U.S. at this time. Virginia was the most populous state.

The expression "not worth a continental" became common, reflecting a distrust of Continental currency.

The first American ship to sail around the world, the *Columbia*, returned to Boston.

1791

politics

Vermont became the fourteenth state.

The Bank of the U.S. was chartered.

Congress passed the first internal revenue law (20¢ to 30¢ per gallon on spirits).

James Buchanan was born in Cove Gap, PA.

Congress established the District of Columbia.

President Washington appointed commissioners to survey the District of Columbia.

Indians launched a surprise attack and routed General St. Clair's expedition to Ohio.

Ten of twelve amendments to the Constitution were ratified. These became the Bill of Rights.

John Quincy Adams was admitted to the Massachusetts Bar.

Protestors of the new whiskey tax staged the Whiskey Insurrection in Pennsylvania (1791-1794).

President Washington initiated the custom of a presidential New Year's Day reception at the Executive Mansion. This practice was suspended by Franklin Roosevelt in 1934.

John Rutledge became the first justice of the U.S. Supreme Court to resign his seat.

The Avery Salt Mine was discovered near New Iberia, LA.

A treaty with the Cherokee Indians was concluded.

President Washington's practice of consulting regularly with his department secretaries gave rise to the presidential "cabinet," an official group of trusted advisors.

science & technology

The first carpet factory was established in Philadelphia.

Coal was discovered in Carbon County, PA.

The first sugar refinery opened in New Orleans.

John Stone patented his pile driver in Concord, MA.

arts & culture

The first historical society in the U.S. was founded in Massachusetts.

The first one-way streets opened in New York City.

1792

politics

Kentucky became the fifteenth state.

The cornerstone for the White House was laid.

Congress passed a law organizing the national militia.

Baltimore, MD dedicated the first memorial to Christopher Columbus.

The national debt at this time stood at $77,227,924.66.

Twenty-four stockbrokers opened the New York Stock Exchange on Wall Street.

The North Carolina state capital was located in Raleigh.

The Republican Party was formed. This party later became the Democratic Party.

Congress authorized the first U.S. mint to be constructed in Philadelphia.

The Bill of Rights went into effect.

A British exploring party led by Vancouver visited San Francisco.

William Henry Harrison was appointed a lieutenant in the Army.

President Washington attempted to reconcile differences between Jefferson and Hamilton.

Vancouver discovered and named Mt. Rainier for Rear Admiral Peter Rainier.

Captain Gray entered the mouth of the Columbia River. This discovery was the basis for the U.S. claim to the Oregon region.

Thomas Pinchney became the first minister to Great Britain under the Constitution.

A treaty of peace was signed with the Wabash and Illinois Indians.

Kentucky adopted its motto, "United we stand, divided we fall."

President Washington signed the first presidential veto.

John Paul Jones, naval hero of the Revolutionary War, died in Paris.

Congress authorized the first U.S. coins to be minted.

science & technology

The first cracker bakery opened in Newburyport, MA.

arts & culture

One of the most popular songs of the day was "O! Dear! What Can the Matter Be?"

New York City held the first Columbus Day celebration in America.

The Female Academy in Philadelphia became the first women's school to receive official sanction.

1793

politics

George Washington was inaugurated in his second term as president, with John Adams as his vice president.

The salary of the president was fixed at $25,000 per year.

Thomas Jefferson's followers assumed the name Republicans.

President Washington declared the U.S. to be neutral in the French and English War.

Some American citizens were granted military commissions by France.

Thomas Jefferson retired as secretary of state.

Stephen F. Austin, known as the Father of Texas, was born in Austinville, VA.

William Henry Harrison joined the army under General Anthony Wayne.

The first U.S. mint was built in Philadelphia.

Middlesex Canal, the first extensive canal in America, was begun. Work on the canal was completed in 1801.

The U.S. and several Indian tribes could not agree on the boundary of the Northwest Territory.

General Wayne moved into Indian country with 2,600 men.

The national debt at this time stood at $80,352,634.04.

science & technology

Eli Whitney applied for a patent on the cotton gin.

The Spanish Company was formed in St. Louis to explore the upper Missouri River and to establish the fur trade.

The first broadcloth was produced in Pittsfield, MA.

John Harrison produced sulphuric acid in Philadelphia.

The first cotton thread was made in Pawtucket, RI.

religion

The first African Church was founded in Philadelphia.

arts & culture

Philadelphia was hit by a yellow fever epidemic.

Kentucky authorized the first state road.

Captain Gray, in the *Columbia*, returned to Boston from his second trip around the world.

1794

politics

science & technology

arts & culture

Two stars were added to the flag for Kentucky and Vermont.

General Wayne ended the Indian War on the Miami River in Ohio.

Congress authorized construction of six warships, thus founding the U.S. Navy which had been defunct since 1775.

Knoxville, TN was established.

John Jay concluded a treaty of amity, commerce, and navigation with the British.

The U.S. Senate ceased its practice of convening behind closed doors.

James Monroe of Virginia was named U.S. minister to France.

Congress prohibited Americans from transporting slaves from one country to another.

Congress approved the Eleventh Amendment to the Constitution. This amendment declared that federal judicial power did not extend for the benefit or protection of individual states in lawsuits brought by American or foreign citizens.

John Quincy Adams was named U.S. minister to The Netherlands.

Captain William Brown discovered Honolulu Harbor, HI.

The first national arsenal was established in Springfield, MA.

The first silver dollar was coined in Philadelphia.

The U.S. Post Office was established.

Eli Whitney was granted a patent for the cotton gin.

The first successful Caesarean operation (surgical removal of an infant from the mother's womb) in the U.S. was performed at Edom, VA.

Benjamin Franklin's autobiography was published.

The first important turnpike in the U.S. was completed between Philadelphia and Lancaster, PA.

Duties were laid on property sold at auction.

President Washington planted the first known alfalfa field in North America.

The Federal Society of Journeymen Cordwainers (shoemakers) was founded in Philadelphia.

The City Hotel was the first hotel built in New York City.

1795

politics

The first coin with the motto "E Pluribus Unum" was issued.

General Wayne signed a treaty with twelve Indian tribes establishing the boundary of southeast Ohio.

John Jay became governor of New York.

The Naturalization Act passed in Congress. This act required a five-year residency before a person could be granted U.S. citizenship.

James K. Polk was born in Pineville, NC.

Alexander Hamilton resigned as secretary of the U.S. Treasury.

John Jay's treaty with Great Britain was ratified by Congress.

The U.S. signed a treaty with Spain establishing territorial boundaries and opening the Mississippi River.

A treaty of friendship, amity and navigation was concluded with Spain.

A national arsenal was established at Harper's Ferry, WV.

Congress repealed taxes on snuff and laid a duty on snuff mills.

President Washington proclaimed a day of Thanksgiving for general benefits.

King Kamehameha conquered the islands of Maui, Lanai, Molokai and Oahu in Hawaii.

The first female federal government employee was hired in Philadelphia.

John Rutledge became the first chief justice of the Supreme Court appointed by the president but not confirmed by the Senate.

James Pickering succeeded Henry Knox as secretary of war.

The first five-cent piece was minted in silver, and was called a half-dime.

Oliver Wolcott was appointed secretary of the treasury.

science & technology

The first primitive railway in the U.S. was built in Boston at about this time.

The first muskets manufactured in the U.S. were produced at the Springfield, MA armory.

The first conveyor belt system was built in Pennsylvania.

The first practical steam engine was built in Philadelphia.

arts & culture

The *New York Prices Current* was the first business publication in New York.

The University of North Carolina became the first college to offer grammar instruction.

1796

politics

Tennessee became the sixteenth state.

President Washington refused to be a candidate for a third term as president.

In his farewell address, President Washington urged the Republic to avoid permanent foreign alliances. Washington's mandate affected foreign policy throughout the next century.

James Monroe was recalled as minister to France.

Thomas Jefferson severed relations with George Washington with the famous Mazzei Letter.

A new treaty with the Creek Indians was concluded by the U.S.

The U.S. concluded a treaty of peace and friendship with Tripoli.

Moses Cleaveland, an agent for the Connecticut Land Company, laid out Cleveland, OH.

The first dimes were put into circulation.

King Kamehameha's attempted invasion of the island of Kauai in Hawaii failed.

Wake Island was discovered in the Pacific.

The first passport was recorded by the State Department.

The British evacuated Detroit and abandoned their fur trading posts on the Great Lakes.

Andrew Jackson was elected to the House of Representatives.

President Washington declared the Jay Treaty with Great Britain in effect.

The first national game law was approved.

The national debt at this time was $83,762,172.07.

science & technology

The first important suspension bridge in America was built in Uniontown, PA.

A nail-cutting and heading machine was patented by George Chandler.

The first pills were patented in the U.S.

religion

The Society for Unitarian Christians was organized.

arts & culture

The Archers, the first opera by an American composer, was produced in New York City.

The Baltimore *Monitor* produced the first Sunday newspaper.

The first elephant in America arrived in New York City.

1797

politics

John Adams was inaugurated as the second president of the U.S. Thomas Jefferson was his vice president.

President Adams was the last Federalist ever to be elected president.

U.S. Navy frigates *Constitution*, *Constellation* and *United States* came into service.

Congress levied a duty on salt.

Asheville, NC was established.

Tennessee adopted the motto, "Agriculture, Commerce."

Congress declared all treaties with France annulled.

James Madison retired from Congress.

President Adams called a special session of Congress to discuss relations with France.

Congress authorized the president to raise a militia of 80,000 men.

Privateering against friendly nations was forbidden by Congress.

William Henry Harrison was made a captain and given command of Fort Washington.

John Quincy Adams was named minister to Prussia.

The Northwest Company established a trading post at Pembina, ND.

The first impeachment proceedings against a U.S. senator (William Blount of Tennessee) were held.

President Adams became the first president to live in Washington, DC.

Andrew Jackson was elected to the U.S. Senate.

New York's state capital moved from New York City to Albany.

The secretary of state reported that 300 U.S. ships had been seized at sea by France.

Congress received the earliest known petition for emancipation by fugitive slaves.

science & technology

The first American patent for a clock was issued to Eli Terry.

Charles Newbold patented the first cast-iron plow.

Nathaniel Briggs patented the first washing machine.

The first glassmaking plant to use coal as fuel was established in Pittsburgh.

The first cryptography chart was published in Philadelphia.

1798

politics

By an act of Congress, the Navy Department was organized.

Benjamin Stoddert was appointed the first secretary of the Navy by President Adams.

Joseph Hopkinson, judge and congressman from Virginia, wrote the patriotic song, "Hail Columbia" which encouraged national support for the war with France.

Congress passed the Alien Act, which granted permission for the U.S. to deport dangerous aliens.

Congress approved an act creating the Mississippi Territory.

John Quincy Adams was sent to negotiate a treaty of commerce with Sweden.

George Washington was appointed general of the U.S. Army in anticipation of war.

Congress passed an act abolishing imprisonment for debts.

Congress approved organization of the U.S. Marine Corps to meet the needs of the naval war with France.

All commercial intercourse between the U.S. and France was suspended.

The U.S. began undeclared war with France.

The U.S. signed a treaty with the Cherokee Indians, in which the Indians ceded land in Tennessee.

Representative Lyon of Vermont became the first congressman to be tried under the Sedition Act for criticizing the president in a campaign speech.

Andrew Jackson became a judge in the Tennessee Superior Court.

William Henry Harrison was named secretary to the Northwest Territory.

The U.S. Public Health Service was organized.

science & technology

Eli Whitney introduced interchangeable parts in manufacturing, which led to mass production.

Betsey Metcalf produced the first straw hats in Rhode Island.

David Wilkinson patented the nut and bolt machine and the first screw.

arts & culture

New York experienced a yellow fever epidemic which caused 2,086 deaths in a population of 50,000.

The first nursing school in the U.S. was established in New York City.

The first encyclopedia published in the U.S. was printed in Philadelphia.

1799

politics

The U.S. frigate *Constellation*, under Commander Truxton, captured a French ship.

Pennsylvania's capital was moved to Lancaster.

Congress voted to raise an army of 40,000 men.

The Sixth U.S. Congress assembled.

James Monroe was elected governor of Virginia.

George Washington died at the age of 67 and was buried at Mt. Vernon, VA. President Adams asked all Americans to wear black crepe armbands for 30 days in memory of the former president.

Patrick Henry, famous for his historic words, "Give me liberty or give me death," died.

Virginia adopted its motto, "Sic Semper Tyrannis" (thus always tyrants).

Georgia adopted the motto "Wisdom, Justice, Moderation."

Frie's Rebellion against the collection of a direct tax began in Pennsylvania.

The term "scab" was first used in reference to strikebreakers in a shoemakers' strike in Philadelphia.

Union "closed shop" rules, which required all employees to be and remain Union members as a condition of employment, appeared in America.

A weights and measures standardization was enacted by Congress.

The U.S. Navy at this time consisted of 42 vessels and 950 guns.

Revenue duties collected for the year amounted to over $13 million.

The national debt at this time amounted to $78,408,669.77.

science & technology

Eliakim Spooner invented the seeding machine.

The first American vessel built on Lake Ontario was assembled in Rochester, NY.

Gold was discovered in the Appalachian Mountains of North Carolina, which came to be known as the Golden State.

arts & culture

The song "Auld Lang Syne" was brought to America from Scotland.

1800

politics

The second U.S. census recorded a population of 5,308,483 in 16 states.

Washington, DC became the new capital of the United States.

Spain ceded the Louisiana Territory to France in a secret treaty.

Millard Fillmore was born in Summer Hill, NY.

The U.S. frigate *Constellation* defeated the French ship *La Vengeance* in a battle at sea.

Congress passed the General Bankruptcy Act, which was repealed in 1802.

Western reserve lands were divided into the Northwest Territory (now Ohio).

Strict laws were enacted to suppress the slave trade.

The government of the District of Columbia was placed in the hands of a board of commissioners.

William Henry Harrison became the territorial governor of Indiana.

St. Louis, MO was founded.

President Adams reached a settlement with France, ending the undeclared naval war.

The Library of Congress was established.

Congress opened its first session in Washington, DC.

President Adams appointed John Marshall to replace Tim Pickering as secretary of state.

science & technology

William Young became the first shoemaker in the U.S. to make individual shoes for the left and right feet.

Samuel Du Pont de Nemours, a friend of Thomas Jefferson, emigrated to the U.S. from France. He later formed the Du Pont Co.

The first fireboat was used in New York.

U.S. cotton plantations exported 35,000 bales of cotton.

The first vaccination for smallpox was given.

The first axe manufacturing plant was erected in New York.

Tea growing was introduced in South Carolina.

religion

The Evangelical Church was founded.

arts & culture

The *National Intelligencer* became the first newspaper published in Washington, DC.

The Santa Rita mines were discovered in New Mexico.

The first known summer theater was established on Broadway in New York City.

1801

politics

Thomas Jefferson was inaugurated as the third president of the U.S. Aaron Burr was his vice president. Jefferson and Burr had tied on electoral votes, so the vote went to the House of Representatives, which elected Jefferson.

President Jefferson became the first president to be inaugurated in Washington, DC.

James Madison became secretary of state. His wife, Dolly Payne Madison, became a great social leader in Washington.

John Marshall became the chief justice of the Supreme Court.

President Jefferson published the first Parliamentary Rules of Order.

Martin Van Buren was admitted to the New York Bar.

John Adams retired to private life in Quincy, MA.

Congress assumed jurisdiction over Washington, DC.

Congress ordered the reduction of the U.S. Navy to 13 ships.

Tripoli declared war on the United States.

The president recalled John Quincy Adams from his position as minister to Prussia.

President Jefferson instituted naval action against Barbary pirates.

The Brooklyn Navy Yard was established in New York.

Benedict Arnold, a traitor to the U.S. during the Revolutionary War, died in exile in London at the age of 60.

science & technology

The first whips made in the U.S. were manufactured in Westfield, MA.

The blowpipe was invented in Pennsylvania.

The first cooperative cheese factory was established in Cheshire, MA.

The Du Pont Co. established a gunpowder plant at Wilmington, DE.

arts & culture

At this time, one American in five was black. By 1860, this proportion was reduced to one in seven.

At receptions given by President Jefferson, guests shook hands with the president. At previous presidential receptions, guests had bowed to the president.

1802

politics

The U.S. military academy at West Point, NY opened on July 4.

John Beckley was named first librarian of Congress.

The war with Tripoli was recognized by Congress.

Washington, DC was incorporated as a city.

James Monroe was appointed minister envoy extraordinary to France.

John Quincy Adams became a state senator in Massachusetts.

Samuel Adams, one of the signers of the Declaration of Independence, died in Massachusetts.

The U.S. Army Corps of Engineers was established.

The internal revenue tax was reduced on domestic spirits and refined sugar.

Congress reenacted the law requiring a five year residency in the U.S. in order to qualify for citizenship.

Boundaries were prescribed for Ohio as the first step toward statehood.

The U.S. entered its fourth economic depression since 1790, this one lasting until 1805.

science & technology

The first sheet copper produced in the U.S. was manufactured in Boston.

The brass industry was begun in Waterbury, CT by Abel Porter & Co.

An early style of upright piano, called the cottage piano, was demonstrated in Philadelphia.

religion

The first Jewish congregation was founded in Philadelphia.

arts & culture

The first U.S. book fair was held in New York City.

About 3% of the population at this time lived in cities. By 1860, this had risen to 15%.

At Blandenburg Dueling Field, five miles from Washington, DC, from 30 to 50 duels were fought between 1802 and 1851.

Chess Made Easy was published in Philadelphia.

1803

politics

Ohio became the seventeenth state.

The U.S. purchased the Louisiana Territory from France for 80 million francs ($15 million), which amounted to about 4¢ per acre.

A treaty with France was ratified by Congress.

Congress authorized the president to take possession of the Louisiana Territory.

Congress passed the Twelfth Amendment to the Constitution, which provided for separate election of the president and vice president.

Captain Bainbridge in the frigate *Philadelphia* struck ground in Tripolitan Harbor and was captured.

Martin Van Buren was admitted to the bar.

John Quincy Adams was elected U.S. senator from Massachusetts.

The Senate approved President Jefferson's plan for an expedition to the West Coast.

James Monroe was named minister to England.

Governor Claiborne of the Mississippi Territory took possession of the Louisiana Territory for the U.S.

Governor Harrison negotiated a treaty with the Indians at Fort Wayne (in what is now Indiana).

The Supreme Court laid down the principle that the Court can render an act of Congress void if the act violates the Constitution.

The first federal judge impeached in the U.S. was John Pickering of New Hampshire.

The Lewis and Clark expedition camped for the winter on Wood River at the mouth of the Missouri River.

science & technology

The apple parer was invented in Pennsylvania.

Glove manufacturing began in Gloversville, NY.

Thomas Moore invented the refrigerator in Baltimore, MD.

Sugar cane was an established crop in Louisiana at this time.

arts & culture

J.J. Audubon of Pennsylvania began banding and tagging birds for study.

A sailors' strike for higher pay in New York was unsuccessful.

The first tax-supported public library was founded in Salisbury, CT.

The first botany book published in the U.S. was printed in Philadelphia.

1804

politics

Franklin Pierce was born in Hillsboro, NH.

Andrew Jackson and his wife built their estate, "the Hermitage," in the Tennessee wilderness.

"Black laws" were enacted in Ohio, requiring the registration of all negroes.

William Dunbar explored the Red River from Natchez, MS.

The Upper Louisiana district was formally transferred to the U.S. by France.

The navy yard was established in Washington, DC.

Lewis and Clark traveled to North Dakota, where they established their winter camp near what is now Bismarck.

William Claiborne was inaugurated governor of Louisiana in New Orleans.

Governor Harrison purchased the land between the Wabash and Ohio Rivers from the Indians.

Stephen Decatur became a national hero for recapturing the *Philadelphia* in Tripoli.

Alexander Hamilton was fatally wounded in a pistol duel with Vice President Aaron Burr.

science & technology

Two patents were granted for "galluses" (suspenders).

Oliver Evans drove a steam-propelled wagon in the streets of Philadelphia.

The first steamboat with a twin-screw propeller was navigated by John Stevens.

The first pontoon bridge was built in Lynn, MA.

Modern printer's ink was brought into use by J. Johnston in Philadelphia.

arts & culture

Bananas were imported to the U.S. for the first time.

Elizabeth Marshall became the first woman pharmacist in Philadelphia.

The first agricultural encyclopedia was published in Philadelphia.

Israel Whelan established the first insurance agency in New York.

1805

politics

Thomas Jefferson was inaugurated for his second term as president.
George Clinton was inaugurated vice president.

At Derna, Tripoli the U.S. flag was raised for the first time over a fort in Europe.

Congress passed an act establishing registration of trademarks.

A treaty of peace and amity was concluded between the U.S. and Tripoli.

Disagreements began with Great Britain which would lead eventually to the War of 1812.

New Orleans, LA was established under American rule.

John Quincy Adams was appointed a professor at Harvard.

James Monroe was sent to Spain on a diplomatic mission.

Congress adopted President Jefferson's plan to negotiate the purchase of Florida.

The city of Detroit was destroyed by fire.

There was a vast resurgence of piracy along U.S. coasts from 1805 to 1825, with more than 3,000 incidents between 1814 and 1824.

Zebulon M. Pike left St. Louis to explore the source of the Mississippi River.

Congress ordered 25 gunboats for the protection of ports and harbors.

With a 16-year-old Shoshone Indian girl named Sacagawea as their guide, Lewis and Clark reached the Pacific Ocean at the mouth of the Columbia River.

The national debt at this time was $82,312,150.50

science & technology

Yale University began offering courses in chemistry.

Robert Fulton built the first marine torpedo.

arts & culture

The term "bronco" was used at this time in reference to hostile Indians. Later the word was applied to wild horses.

1806

politics

Congress authorized the first federal highway to run from Cumberland, MD to the Ohio River.

The British vessel *Leander* fired upon the American ship *Richard*.

Henry Clay became a U.S. senator from Kentucky.

The city of Detroit was rebuilt.

A policy of "partial nonintercourse," suspension of trade relations with England, was adopted.

England claimed the right to search American ships on the high seas. The U.S. objected.

Aaron Burr, the former vice president, schemed to set up a government in Spanish Mexico.

Andrew Jackson killed Charles Dickinson in a duel in New Jersey.

Lewis and Clark returned to St. Louis.

Congress appropriated $2 million to purchase Florida and Texas to the Colorado River.

American trade was injured when Napoleon, the Emperor of France, ordered a blockade of Great Britain.

Zebulon M. Pike first saw Pike's Peak (CO) on November 15.

James Monroe and William Pinckney were selected to settle the U.S. dispute with England.

Congress passed the Non-Importation Act, prohibiting the importation of British goods.

science & technology

Gas street lighting was introduced in the U.S. at Newport, RI.

William Colgate became the first soap manufacturer to render fats in his New York plant.

The first cider mill was patented in Stanfield, CT.

religion

The cornerstone was laid for the first cathedral in Baltimore, MD.

arts & culture

Noah Webster published his *Compendious Dictionary of the English Language.*

The Pennsylvania Academy of Fine Arts was incorporated in Philadelphia.

The *Literary Cabinet*, published at Yale, became the first college magazine in the U.S.

The first stories of George Washington and the cherry tree began to appear.

President Jefferson's grandson, James Madison Randolf, was the first child to be born in the White House.

Russian ships arrived in San Francisco to collect food for starving Russians.

1807

politics

Congress passed an act prohibiting African slave trade after January 1, 1808.

Robert E. Lee was born in Westmoreland, VA.

British ships were ordered out of all American waters.

The duty on salt was repealed.

John Tyler graduated from William & Mary College.

Aaron Burr's political career was ended because of his slaying of Alexander Hamilton in a duel.

The U.S. experienced a minor economic depression, which lasted until 1810.

Aaron Burr was tried for treason and acquitted.

Congress authorized the building of 188 gunboats, raising the total to 257.

The British warship *Leopard* fired on the U.S. frigate *Chesapeake*.

The British announced that they would pursue their policy of impressing (forcing civilians into military service) Americans even more vigorously.

The national debt at this time was $69,218,398.64.

science & technology

Robert Fulton's steamboat *Clermont* made its first run in New York.

Manuel Lisa built a trading post at the mouth of the Big Horn River in what is now Montana and organized the fur trade in the areas of Montana, Ikaho, Washington, Wyoming and Nebraska.

Stephen Whitney built a railway on Beacon Hill in Boston.

The first successful flint glass factory was established in Philadelphia.

The first glue factory was established in Boston.

The first lifeboat was built in Nantucket, MA.

religion

The U.S. Evangelical Association, founded by Jacob Albright, held its first convention.

arts & culture

The first soft drink (soda pop) was prepared in Philadelphia.

The first sheep exhibition was held in Pittsfield, MA.

New York City established the first school for the deaf.

1808

politics	science & technology	religion	arts & culture

politics

Napoleon ordered all U.S. ships in French ports seized.

The first recorded duel between congressmen occurred at Bladensburg, MD.

Zachary Taylor entered the army as a first lieutenant.

James Monroe returned to the U.S. from his European mission.

John Quincy Adams resigned his seat in the Senate.

The Osage Treaty was signed. The Osage Indians ceded nearly all of what is now Missouri and Arkansas north of the Missouri River and moved to the reservation along the Arkansas River in what is now Oklahoma.

Andrew Johnson was born in Raleigh, N.C.

Because of an embargo on foreign trade, the price of wheat dropped from $2.00 to 75¢ per bushel.

science & technology

John J. Astor established the American Fur Co., with headquarters on Mackinac Island, and soon established a monopoly on Canadian fur.

The St. Louis Fur Co. was organized.

Fur trading began in Idaho at Bonners Ferry.

John Stevens' steamboat, *Phoenix,* made its first trip from Hoboken to Philadelphia.

The first brush manufacturing business opened in Medford, MA.

religion

The first bible society in the U.S. was founded in Philadelphia.

arts & culture

New Orleans became known as the operatic capital of America.

Harvard University formed the first college orchestra in the U.S.

The Indian Princess was the first play about an Indian to be written by an American.

The American Academy of Fine Arts was founded in New York.

The first temperance society in th U.S. was formed at Moreau, NY.

The *Missouri Gazette* in St. Louis became the first newspaper west of the Mississippi River.

The American Law Journal was first published in Baltimore.

Pigtails for men went out of fashion at about this time.

1809

politics

James Madison was inaugurated as the fourth president. George Clinton was his vice president.

Thomas Paine died in New York at the age of 72.

The first inaugural ball was held.

George Clinton became the first vice president to serve under two different presidents.

Thomas Jefferson retired to Monticello, his home in VA, after 44 years of continuous public service.

James Buchanan graduated from Dickinson College in Pennsylvania.

John Tyler was admitted to the Virginia Bar.

James Monroe was named secretary of state.

John Quincy Adams was named minister to Russia.

Abraham Lincoln was born in Hodgenville, KY.

Pennsylvania adopted the motto "Virtue, Liberty, and Independence."

Illinois was established as a separate territory from the Indiana Territory.

New York adopted the motto "Excelsior."

science & technology

The *Accommodation* became the first steamboat on the St. Lawrence River.

Moses Rogers became the first person to navigate a steamboat in open sea when he sailed from New York to Philadelphia.

Luther Goddard made the first clock in Shrewbury, CT.

Mary Kies was the first woman to be granted a patent in the U.S.

The first railroad for freight transport was established in Pennsylvania.

Ephraim McDowell performed the first abdominal surgical operation in Kentucky.

At this time there were 109 cotton mills in New England, compared to a total of one in 1790.

The first screw-cutting machines were designed and produced in Massachusetts.

religion

The first Hebrew dictionary in America was published in New York.

The Christian church, Disciples of Christ, was organized in Pennsylvania.

The first Catholic magazine in English was issued in Detroit.

arts & culture

Washington Irving wrote the story "The Legend of Sleepy Hollow."

The first U.S. cricket club was founded in Boston.

At this time there were 30 daily newspapers in the U.S.

1810

politics	*science & technology*	*religion*	*arts & culture*

politics

The third U.S. Census recorded a total population of 7,239,881 in the 17 states.

Napoleon continued seizing U.S. ships in French ports.

At this time, the region northwest of Ohio had only 31,000 inhabitants.

The earliest American fort in the Pacific Northwest was built near what is now St. Anthony, ID.

The island of Kauai in Hawaii was ceded to King Kamehameha.

Indians drove settlers from the lead mines and colony of Dubuque, IA.

Zachary Taylor became a captain in the Army.

Inhabitants of western Florida revolted and captured the fort at Baton Rouge, LA.

The national debt at this time was $53,173,217.52.

science & technology

The first metal pens were manufactured in Baltimore.

The North West Fur Co. established a small settlement near what is now Spokane, WA.

The first carpet factory was started in Frederick City, MD.

The first silk mill was established at Mansfield, CT.

The mailbox was invented by Thomas Brown.

religion

Alexander Campbell and his son Thomas founded the Campbellite Church of Christ.

arts & culture

The first regular orchestra in the U.S. was organized in Boston.

The first Irish magazine, *The Shamrock*, was published in New York.

The first unofficial heavyweight boxing champion of the U.S., Tom Molineaux, was beaten in a 40-round fight in England.

The first horse breeding society was founded in Boston.

1811

politics

William Henry Harrison led troops to a victory over Indian Chief Tecumseh at Tippecanoe River in Indiana. This victory would inspire his 1840 presidential campaign slogan "Tippecanoe and Tyler, Too."

The U.S. frigate *President* defeated the British ship *Little Belt*.

A second war with the Northwest Indians began. This war would continue until 1813.

The U.S. seized western Florida over British protests.

John J. Astor established the city of Astoria in what is now Oregon to supply the Alaskan Territory.

Fort Harrison was completed on the Wabash River.

Trading posts were first established among the Indians.

A bounty of $16 was offered to army recruits, along with three months' extra pay and 160 acres of land upon discharge.

The first filibuster (obstructionist tactic intended to delay legislative action) occurred in the U.S. Senate.

The first naval hospital was authorized.

John Tyler was elected to the Virginia legislature.

This was the first year that U.S. exports exceeded imports.

Henry Clay was elected to the House of Representatives.

The national debt at this time was $48,005,587.76.

science & technology

The first steamboat sailed down the Mississippi River, arriving in New Orleans on January 12.

A Pacific Fur Co. expedition explored the valley of the Snake River.

arts & culture

The *Free Masons' Magazine* was first published in Philadelphia.

The first educational magazine in the U.S., the *Juvenile Mirror*, was published in New York.

The worst earthquake in American history rocked the Ohio and Mississippi valleys.

Regular steamboat service began on the Mississippi River between New Orleans and Natchez.

The Knickerbocker Boat Club was organized in New York City.

The first news agency was established in Boston.

Fashionable ladies of this time used rouge and pearl powder on their faces.

1812

politics

The U.S. declared war against Great Britain.

Louisiana became the eighteenth state.

Congress authorized the first issuance of U.S. war bonds.

The U.S. ship *Old Ironsides* defeated the British ships *Guerriere* and *Java*.

The U.S. Army raised a force of 36,700 men.

General Hull led Americans into Canada and was defeated at Mackinaw.

Captain Zachary Taylor defended Fort Harrison, IN.

The Algonquin Indians joined the British side in the war.

President Madison refused the services of Andrew Jackson, so Jackson organized an independent military corps.

American privateers began to prey on British commerce.

Congress placed an embargo on American shipping.

The Seminole War was fought in Florida.

Martin Van Buren became a New York state senator.

The General Land Office was established.

Detroit surrendered to the British.

Colonel John Stevens of New Jersey designed the armor plate for ships.

Congress passed the first Foreign Aid Act for Venezuelan earthquake victims.

President Madison was authorized to call up 100,000 men for six month service terms.

In New York, a mass meeting was held to protest the war.

As Louisiana was now the name of a state, the former Louisiana Territory was renamed the Missouri Territory.

The national debt at this time amounted to $45,209,737.90.

science & technology

Ben Rush, known as the father of American psychiatry, wrote *Diseases of the Mind*.

Donald Mackenzie established a winter trading post at Lewiston, ID.

The first file-making machine was invented in Greenfield, MA.

arts & culture

Samuel Wilson, a meat packer from Troy, NY, became the original Uncle Sam.

1813

politics

President Madison was inaugurated for his second term. Elbridge Gerry was his vice president.

The British ship *Peacock* was captured by the U.S. ship *Hornet*, and the British *Boxer* was taken by the U.S. *Enterprise*.

The Peoria Indian War was fought in Illinois.

The British attempted to blockade the Atlantic coast.

Captain Lawrence of the *Chesapeake* cried the famous words, "Don't give up the ship."

The Creek Indian War of 1813-1814 was fought in Alabama.

Buffalo, NY was completely destroyed by British and Indian soldiers.

At the Battle of Lake Erie, O.H. Perry spoke the famous words, "We have met the enemy and they are ours."

Congress appropriated $2.5 million for building warships.

The American General Dearborn captured Ft. George on the Niagara River.

General Zebulon Pike was killed in a raid on Toronto, Canada.

Shawnee Indian Chief Tecumseh, who was named a brigadier general by the British, was killed in fighting against U.S. troops.

Russia offered to mediate between the U.S. and Great Britain to end the war.

Congress limited the U.S. Army to 58,000 men.

The national debt at this time was $55,692,827.57.

science & technology

George Stephenson built his first locomotive.

Jethro Wood patented the iron plow.

religion

The Baptist mission in Burma was founded.

The first religious weekly in the U.S., the *Religious Remembrancer*, was founded in Philadelphia.

arts & culture

"Tis the Last Rose of Summer" was a popular song at this time.

The dice game "craps" was introduced in the U.S. in New Orleans. The name evolved from "Johnny Crapaud," a nickname for Louisiana Creoles.

By this time, running water and plumbing were installed in the White House.

1814

politics

General Andrew Jackson defeated Chief Weatherford in the Creek Indian War, forcing the Creeks to cede two-thirds of their vast territory *(present day Georgia and Alabama)* to the U.S.

The British captured Washington, DC and set fire to the Capitol Building, the White House and the Navy Yard in retaliation for U.S. troops burning the capital in upper Canada.

All government buildings in Washington, DC were burned except the patent office.

Alexandria, VA was saved from destruction by a payment of $100,000 to the British.

Congress convened meetings in the patent office after the city was burned.

General Ross landed at Patuxent River, MD with 4,500 British troops.

Congress increased the army to 63,000 regulars.

Major Zachary Taylor was driven from Credit Island near what is now Davenport, IA.

Congress increased the bounty to army volunteers to $124 and 320 acres.

The British blockade extended along the entire U.S. Atlantic coast.

The first wartime conscription bill, enrolling men for compulsory military service, was passed by the Senate.

General Jackson captured Pensacola, FL and put New Orleans under martial law.

Commander MacDonough defeated the British fleet on Lake Champlain.

Congress authorized a $25 million loan and $10 million in treasury notes.

A convention was held in Montreal to arrange for an exchange of prisoners of war between the U.S. and England.

President Madison received a proposal for negotiations and accepted it.

A treaty of peace was signed with Great Britain at Ghent, Belgium on December 24.

The national debt at this time was $81,487,846.24.

science & technology

The first steam-powered warship, the *Demologos*, was launched at New York.

The first factory in the world to manufacture cloth by machine power was built at Waltham, MA.

The first circular saw was produced in Bentonville, NY.

arts & culture

The "Star Spangled Banner" was written by Francis Scott Key by the light of artillery fire while he was detained by the British.

1815

politics

The Battle of New Orleans was fought two weeks after the Treaty of Ghent, which officially ended the War of 1812 between the U.S. and Great Britain, was signed.

Congress declared war against Algeria for molesting American ships.

Captain Stephen Decatur left New York for Algiers with 10 ships.

The cornerstone for the first public monument to Washington was laid at Baltimore.

Captain Decatur captured the Algerian ships *Mashouda* and *Estido.*

The U.S. signed a treaty with Algeria.

The U.S. Army was reduced to 10,000 men.

General Jackson was fined $1,000 for contempt of court in New Orleans after refusing to honor a writ of habeas corpus.

The estimated cost of the war with England came to $200 million.

The library of Thomas Jefferson sold more than 7,000 volumes to the Library of Congress.

President Madison proclaimed a day of thanksgiving for peace.

There was a severe economic depression in the U.S. from 1815 to 1821.

John Quincy Adams was named minister to Great Britain.

The Board of Navy Commissioners was established.

The U.S. signed treaties with Indians who were allied with the British during the war.

The first naval officers' training school was established in Boston.

In gratitude for his help at the Battle of New Orleans, President Madison pardoned pirate Jean Lafitte.

Lafitte then resumed piracy from Galveston, TX.

The government raised funds by taxing watches, hats, caps and boots.

The national debt at this time amounted to $119,600,000.00.

science & technology

The patent medicine business developed rapidly in the U.S. from 1815-1860.

arts & culture

Barnstorming, a term later used to refer to airplane stunt pilots, originally was the name of a theatrical troup from Lexington, KY, whose members often slept in barns.

The first music festival was held in Boston.

The first pacifist society in the U.S. (the New York Peace Society) was organized in New York City.

1816

politics

Indiana became the nineteenth state.

Columbus was made the capital of Ohio.

Congress appropriated $1 million a year for eight years to increase the efficiency of the Navy.

Treaties of friendship and commerce were completed with Sweden and Norway.

Martin Van Buren was named New York's state attorney general while still serving as a state senator.

William Henry Harrison and John Tyler were elected to Congress.

Abraham Lincoln moved from Kentucky to Indiana.

The Seminole Indian uprising was quelled in Florida.

Daniel Webster began promoting free trade.

A treaty of peace and amity was signed with Algeria.

A demand of the "Holy Alliance" by Russia, Austria and Prussia for the abolition of the republics in South America liberated by Bolivar was the first step toward the Monroe Doctrine.

The national debt at this time was $127,335.000.00, or about $15 per person.

science & technology

The first savings bank in the U.S. was organized in Boston.

The *Ontario*, the first steamship on the Great Lakes, was built in New York.

The first iron wire suspension bridge was built over Schuylkill River.

The first boiler plates were manufactured in Coatesville, PA.

Work was begun in New York on the Champlain Canal.

The first hand printing press constructed in America was built in Philadelphia.

religion

The first national bible society was organized in New York.

arts & culture

The familiar phrase "Our country, right or wrong" was incorrectly quoted from a toast by Stephen Decatur, who said, "Our country, in her intercourse with foreign nations may she always be in the right and always successful, right or wrong."

1817

politics

James Monroe was inaugurated as the fifth president. Daniel D. Tompkins was his vice president.

Mississippi became the twentieth state.

The Seminole War of 1817-1818 began. General Jackson was assigned to head the American forces.

John Quincy Adams was named secretary of state.

James Madison retired to Montpelier, VA.

The U.S. entered a prosperous period known as the "Era of Good Feelings."

Baltimore Quakers petitioned Congress to protect Negro slaves against kidnapping.

Fort Smith, AR was established to preserve order among nearby Indians.

The New York Stock Exchange was formally organized.

The Rush-Bagot Agreement

demilitarized the Great Lakes.

The eastern part of the Mississippi Territory became the Alabama Territory.

Pirate Jean Lafitte occupied Galveston Island on the Gulf Coast.

Massachusetts became the first state to enact a game law.

John Tyler was elected to the House of Representatives.

Thousands of settlers moved west at this time and the prairies were dotted with log cabins.

science & technology

The first insane asylum in the U.S. was established in Frankford, PA.

Baltimore, MD was the first city to inaugurate a gas company for lighting the streets.

Construction of the Erie Canal was begun in New York.

Ft. Pierre, SD was founded as a fur trading post.

The first iron mill to puddle and roll iron was built in Brownsville, PA

religion

The San Rafael mission was founded in northern California.

arts & culture

The first theater showboat left Nashville, TN.

A cholera epidemic spread across Atlanta, causing over a million deaths.

The Harvard Law School was established.

1818

politics

Illinois became the twenty-first state.

The fall of Pensacola, FL to General Andrew Jackson ended the Seminole War.

The Executive Mansion was restored in Washington, DC after the fire of 1814. It was painted white to cover the scorch marks, and thus earned the name the White House.

Illinois adopted the motto "State sovereignty—national unity."

Congress passed the Pension Act, thus beginning the pension system.

An American polar expedition was sent out.

The Academy of Natural Sciences was founded.

James K. Polk graduated from the University of North Carolina.

All lands east of the Continental Divide were ceded to the U.S. by

Great Britain. Both countries claimed the lands west of the divide.

A treaty of commerce was completed with Great Britain.

Congress established that the flag of the U.S. should contain 13 red and white stripes and white stars on a blue field.

The Army Medical Corps was organized. The first surgeon general was J. Lovell.

Illinois adopted a state constitution prohibiting slavery.

Connecticut adopted a state constitution replacing its former royal charter.

Petitions from Missouri asking for statehood were presented to Congress.

Paul Revere died in Boston at the age of 83.

The national debt at this time was $103,466,633.83.

science & technology

The first patent leather manufactured in the U.S. was produced in Newark, NJ.

Steam was first used for heating purposes.

The first chair factory was established at Riverton, CT.

The Lehigh Navigation Co. was formed to mine coal in Pennsylvania.

The first natural cement rock was discovered at Fayetteville, NY.

religion

The American Bible Society was founded.

arts & culture

A crusade was begun in New York City to keep pigs off the streets.

1819

politics

Alabama became the twenty-second state. This meant that there were 11 free states and 11 slave states in the Union at this time.

The first immigration law was enacted by Congress.

The U.S. and England signed an agreement for the occupation of the territory of Oregon.

The U.S. bought the territory of Florida from Spain for $5,499,768.00.

Congress separated the territories of Arkansas and Missouri.

Congress authorized the Navy to suppress the slave trade.

The city of Indianapolis, IN was settled.

Discussions began between the North and South on the issue of slavery.

An expedition set off to explore the Yellowstone region.

Fort Snelling, MN was established as part of the frontier defense.

King Kamehameha died in Hawaii.

The U.S. suffered a slight economic depression.

The first American whaling ships visited Hawaii.

The boundaries of North Carolina, South Carolina, and Georgia were set.

The Cherokee Indians ceded a large tract of land to North Carolina.

The Massachusetts legislature separated Maine from Massachusetts.

President Monroe was authorized to take possession of east and west Florida and to establish a government there.

science & technology

The first American steamboat to cross the Atlantic left Savannah, GA.

The first silk thread was manufactured in Connecticut.

The first bicycle was patented in New York.

The first angle iron was manufactured in Pittsburgh, PA.

arts & culture

Washington Irving's stories "Rip Van Winkle" and "The Legend of Sleepy Hollow" were published.

The first tightrope act was performed in New York City.

Thomas Jefferson established the University of Virginia, the first university which required religious affiliation of its faculty.

Corsets came into use at about this time.

1820

politics

Maine became the twenty-third state.

The population of the 23 states at this time was 9,638,453.

Major Stephen Long left Pittsburgh to explore south of the Missouri River and the Rocky Mountains.

A total of 8,385 immigrants arrived in the U.S.

By this time approximately 250,000 immigrants had arrived in the U.S. since 1789.

Henry Clay resigned as speaker of the House of Representatives.

Montgomery, AL was established.

Zachary Taylor moved from Kentucky to Louisiana.

Congress organized its first committee on agriculture.

The Missouri Compromise was enacted admitting Missouri as a slave state, Maine as a free state and prohibiting slavery in the northern part of the Louisiana Purchase.

The capital of Alabama was moved to Cahaba.

The Magee-Kearney Expedition moved up the Missouri River toward Yellowstone.

The population of the region north and west of Ohio was estimated at 200,000. In 1810 it had been only 31,000.

The *Mayflower of Liberia* set sail from New York for Sierra Leone with 86 Negroes aboard to settle colonies in Africa.

The capital of Illinois was moved to Vandalia.

A new charter for Washington, DC allowed for the mayor to be selected by the people.

Governor Cass from Detroit discovered the source of the Mississippi River and named it Lake Cass.

The cornerstone for Fort Snelling in Minnesota was laid.

Daniel Boone died at the age of 85.

The national debt at this time amounted to $91,015,566.15.

science & technology

U.S. cotton plantations exported 320,000 bales of cotton.

Gas was first used for street lights in the U.S. in Baltimore, MD.

A grasshopper plague destroyed crops along the northern Red River.

The first steamboat line between New York and New Orleans was established.

Cranberries were first cultivated in Dennis, MA.

religion

The first corps of American missionaries arrived in Hawaii.

arts & culture

Pike's Peak was first ascended by Edwin James.

The first anti-slavery magazine, *The Emancipator*, was published in Tennessee.

Men's watch fobs were a fashion necessity.

1821

politics

President Monroe was inaugurated for his second term. Daniel D. Tompkins was his vice president.

Missouri was admitted as the twenty-fourth state.

Debtors' prisons were abolished in Kentucky.

The Santa Fe Trail, an important trade route between Independence, MO and Santa Fe, NM, was opened by William Becknell.

A total of 9,127 immigrants arrived in the U.S.

President Monroe appointed Andrew Jackson of Tennessee to be governor of Florida.

Martin Van Buren was elected to the U.S. Senate.

Spanish authorities in Mexico granted Moses Austin the right to settle 300 families in Texas. Austin died soon after and his son Stephen inherited the grants.

Russia sought to exclude foreign ships from Alaska.

The Maine legislature passed a liquor licensing law.

Mexico gained independence from Spain.

The N.B. Palmer Expedition, which discovered Antarctica in 1820, returned to the U.S.

American troops gained possession of the Spanish fort at St. Augustine, FL.

The national debt at this time was $89,987,427.66.

science & technology

The first iron sea-going vessel was constructed.

The Hudson Bay Co. absorbed the Northwest Co., creating a monopoly of the Columbia River fur trade.

The first natural gas drilled in the U.S. came from a well in Fredonia, NY.

The first firehose of rubber-lined cotton web was used in Boston.

arts & culture

James Fenimore Cooper published *The Spy.*

The *Saturday Evening Post* was founded.

The first high school in the U.S. opened in Boston.

Coffee came into general use in America at about this time.

The term "cowboy" came into use as settlers pushed west and discovered Mexican ranches in what is now Texas.

Ladies shoes began to be visible under decidedly shorter skirts.

1822

politics

Ulysses S. Grant was born in Point Pleasant, OH.

Rutherford B. Hayes was born in Delaware, OH.

The Federal Party was disbanded.

Florida was made a U.S. territory.

Missouri adopted the motto "Salus Populi Supreme Lex Esto" ("The welfare of the people is the supreme law.")

William Becknell drove the first wagon from western Missouri to Santa Fe.

Spanish rule ended in California and Mexican rule began.

Stephen Austin arrived in Mexico to obtain the Texas land grant.

The U.S. recognized the republics of Chile, Columbia and Peru.

The headwaters of the Rio Grande River were explored by Jacob Fowler.

The Tennessee legislature nominated Andrew Jackson for president.

The Kentucky legislature proposed Henry Clay for president.

The U.S. recognized the nationhood of Mexico.

The Mississippi legislature held its first meeting at Le Fleur's Bluff (now Jackson).

science & technology

The first patent for false teeth was issued to C.M. Graham.

The journeymen hatters went on strike in New York City.

James and McKnight were the first traders over the Santa Fe Trail.

The first fireproof building was constructed in Charleston, SC.

A 280-mile section of the Erie Canal opened between Rochester and Albany, NY.

The "mountain men," including Jedediah Smith and others, took over the fur operations in the northern Rocky Mountains.

The first quinine was manufactured in Philadelphia.

The first treadmill was completed in New York City.

religion

The first printing in Hawaii was done by missionaries.

arts & culture

Washington Irving wrote *Bracebridge Hall*.

The first horticultural society was incorporated in New York.

Football was prohibited at Yale University. Violators were fined a half-dollar.

1823

politics

The Monroe Doctrine, a statement of U.S. opposition to colonization and interference with independent nations in the Western Hemisphere, was proposed by President Monroe in a speech to Congress.

A total of 6,354 immigrants arrived in the U.S.

Andrew Jackson was elected to the U.S. Senate from Tennessee.

James K. Polk was elected to the Tennessee House of Representatives.

John Tyler was elected to the House of Delegates in Virginia.

Battles were fought with Blackfeet and Arickara Indians.

General Long's survey expedition designated to official boundary between the U.S. and Canada.

Colonel Leavenworth, from a post at Council Bluffs (present day IA),

led troops that defeated the Arickara Indians.

Memphis, TN was established.

The first U.S. diplomatic ministers were sent to South American nations.

The Jones-Immel exploration party was massacred on the Yellowstone River.

The national debt at this time was $90,875,877.28.

science & technology

The first locomotive to pull a train ran in Hoboken, NJ.

The *Virginia* was the first steamboat to navigate the upper Mississippi River. Eventually, over 2,500 steamboats would provide service to settlers on the Mississippi.

The Delaware & Hudson Railroad was chartered.

New York's Champlain Canal opened between the Hudson River and Lake Champlain.

The first strike in which women participated took place in Pawtucket, RI.

religion

Joseph Smith claimed to have a vision of the holy tablets of the *Book of Mormon*.

The first Catholic priest to serve in Congress was elected from the Michigan Territory.

arts & culture

"Home Sweet Home" was first sung in America at Park Theater in New York.

James Fenimore Cooper wrote *The Pioneers*, the first of his "Leather-Stocking" novels.

The first rhyming dictionary was published in New York.

The first big horse racing event in America took place in Long Island, NY with a purse of $20,000.00

1824

politics

A treaty with Russia fixed the north boundary of Oregon at 54°40', which left the land west of the Rockies in dispute between the U.S. and Great Britain. The popular slogan "fifty-four forty or fight" referred to this dispute.

Mountain man Jedediah Smith found a gateway through the Rocky Mountains.

T.J. (Stonewall) Jackson was born in Clarksburg, VA.

Revolutionary war hero General Lafayette, now 67 years old, revisited the U.S. and toured all 24 states. Congress voted him $200,000.00 and a township in any unoccupied land he selected.

Russia signed a treaty with the U.S. to allow American ships to sail to Alaska.

The U.S. signed a treaty allowing Russians to hunt in the Oregon Territory.

Henry Clay introduced his "American System"

of economic development and domestic improvement.

The Great Salt Lake in Utah was discovered by James Bridger, a 20-year-old trooper.

Indianapolis, IN was established.

King Kamehameha II and Queen Kamemalu of Hawaii died in London.

The name "National Guard" was first used by a New York unit.

Mexico created a territory in what is now the southwestern U.S.

The Bureau of Indian Affairs was created.

The election of John Quincy Adams for president ended the "Virginia dynasty" created by the successive election of presidents from VA: Washington, Jefferson, Madison and Monroe.

Jedediah Smith discovered a south pass to Oregon.

The states of Tejas and Coahuila were formed under the new constitution of Mexico.

The U.S. recognized the nationhood of Brazil.

William Henry Harrison was elected to the Senate.

The city of Tallahasse became the capital of the Florida Territory.

science & technology

The Chesapeake & Ohio Canal Co. was formed.

The first engineering college was founded in Troy, NY.

The first rubber galoshes were advertised in Boston at $5 a pair.

religion

The first black woman was admitted to a Catholic convent in Loretto, KY.

arts & culture

The first reformatory for juveniles was incorporated in New York City.

1825

politics

The first overland expedition to California was made by Jedediah Smith. His route from the Great Salt Lake became a major traffic artery during the 1849 gold rush.

Jefferson Barracks, MO was established by the War Department.

Samuel Houston was inaugurated as president of the Republic of Texas.

Sing Sing prison in New York was built.

William Morgan's abduction and murder led to the organization of the Anti-Mason Party in New York.

Pennsylvania became the first state to institute a state inheritance tax.

Both Thomas Jefferson and John Adams died on July 4, the fiftieth anniversary of the Declaration of Independence.

science & technology

A rivalry between British and American fur hunters prevailed during the 1820s and 1830s.

The first internal combustion engine was patented by Sam Morey in Oxford, NH.

John Stevens built the first steam locomotive in Hoboken, NJ.

The first telegraph poles were erected at Union Racetrack, Long Island, NY.

The first cloth-covered button was made in Easthampton, MA.

The Mohawk & Hudson Railroad was chartered.

arts & culture

Samuel Woodworth wrote the poem "The Old Oaken Bucket."

James Fenimore Cooper published *The Last of the Mohicans*.

The first New York City performance of Shakespeare's *A Midsummer Night's Dream* was produced.

J.H. Hackett became the first American actor to appear abroad.

The American Society for the Promotion of Temperance (abstinence from liquor) was founded in Boston.

J.B. Russworm became the first black college graduate at Brunswick, ME.

The Academy of National Design was founded in New York.

The first high school for girls was established in Boston.

Harvard University initiated gymnastics instruction.

1826

politics

John Quincy Adams was inaugurated as the sixth president. John C. Calhoun was his vice president.

Joel R. Poinsett was named the first minister to Mexico.

The U.S. ratified a treaty establishing the U.S./Russian boundary line.

Henry Clay was named U.S. Secretary of State.

The Creek Indians killed their own Chief McIntosh for making a treaty with the U.S. ceding territory in Georgia and Alabama.

John Tyler was elected governor of Virginia.

James K. Polk was elected to the U.S. Congress.

The city of Akron, OH was laid out.

The Osage Indians signed a treaty at Council Grove, KS granting the right-of-way for the Santa Fe Trail.

Lafayette laid the cornerstone of the Bunker Hill Monument in Boston.

The first known Norwegians in America arrived in New York.

The Santa Fe Trail was surveyed by the government.

The national debt at this time was $83,788,432.71.

science & technology

Over 600 carpenters in Boston went on strike demanding a 10-hour work day.

The Erie Canal officially opened in New York.

The first small hotel was erected at Coney Island, N.Y.

The Columbia Fur Co. initiated the buffalo skin trade in the U.S.

The United Tailoresses of New York became the first American trade union for women only.

The first firebrick was manufactured in Woodbridge, NJ.

arts & culture

Italian opera was introduced in the U.S. at Park Theater in New York City.

The first U.S. gymnasium opened in Northampton, MA.

Covered wagon caravan traffic on the Great Plains existed from about 1825 to 1875.

1827

politics

Fort Leavenworth was built in Kansas. It later became the first incorporated town in Kansas.

A joint occupation of Oregon was agreed upon by the U.S. and Great Britain.

A total of 18,875 immigrants arrived in the U.S.

The state of New York abolished slavery.

Ft. Union, MT was settled by Americans.

John Tyler was elected to the U.S. Senate from Virginia.

Mexico made California a Mexican province.

The first printed laws were published in Hawaii.

The U.S. experienced its eighth economic depression since 1790.

The U.S. made an unsuccessful attempt to purchase Texas from Mexico.

The governor of Georgia called out the state militia to resist U.S. troops in a dispute over the surveying of Creek Indian lands.

The national debt at this time was $73,987,357.20.

science & technology

Aluminum was discovered.

The Baltimore & Ohio Railroad was chartered. At this time the trains were horse-drawn cars.

The first telegraph was constructed.

The first successful silk mill was established in Gurleyville, CT which began a craze for raising mulberry trees to feed the silkworms.

The first lithographic printing establishment was completed in Boston.

religion

Mexico expelled all Franciscans from what is now Arizona and New Mexico, thus ending the mission era.

arts & culture

Mme. Francisque Hutin introduced ballet to the U.S. in New York.

The first poetry of Edgar Allan Poe was printed in Boston.

The first kindergarten was established in New York City.

The first Mardi Gras was celebrated in New Orleans.

Freedom's Journal, the first black newspaper in the U.S., was published in New York City.

The first public swimming pool opened in Boston.

1828

politics

The Democratic Party was formed as an extension of the Republican Party, which was organized in 1792.

The total value of gold mined in the U.S. to this time was $110,000. It was extracted from small deposits in North Carolina.

Martin Van Buren was elected governor of New York.

A total of 27,382 immigrants arrived in the U.S.

William Henry Harrison was the first foreign minister to Colombia.

Gold deposits were found in Georgia.

Louisville, KY was incorporated as a city.

The first strike in which the militia was called out took place in Paterson, NJ.

The Michigan territorial capital was established at Detroit.

Mechanics in Philadelphia established a workingman's (state) political party.

Vice President Calhoun resigned in protest of a new tariff bill.

The national debt at this time amounted to $67,475,043.87.

science & technology

Construction began on the B & O Railroad.

Ground was broken for the Chesapeake & Ohio Canal.

Peter Cooper founded his famous iron works in Baltimore, MD.

The first brake was patented by Robert Turner in Ward, MA.

The first manufacturers' fair was held in New York City.

Joseph Henry invented the electric magnet in Albany, NY.

Paul Moody first used belts of leather in transmitting power in Lowell, MA.

Tremont House in Boston became the first hotel to install indoor bathrooms.

arts & culture

Noah Webster's *American Dictionary of the English Language* was published.

The first theatrical version of *Rip Van Winkle* was presented in Albany, NY.

James Fenimore Cooper wrote *The Red Rover*.

The first U.S. archery club was formed in Philadelphia.

The first women's temperance society was organized in Ohio.

The first Indian newspaper, the *Cherokee Phoenix*, was published in New Echota, GA.

1829

politics

Andrew Jackson was inaugurated as the seventh president of the U.S. John C. Calhoun was his vice president.

The American Society for Encouraging Settlement of the Oregon Territory was established in Boston.

A total of 22,520 immigrants arrived in the U.S.

Martin Van Buren was named U.S. Secretary of State.

Englishman James Smithson bequeathed to the U.S. $600,000.00 to build the Smithsonian Institution in Washington, DC.

The U.S. and Austria concluded a treaty of commerce and navigation.

The term "kitchen cabinet" was used to identify a group of unofficial confidants of President Jackson.

David E. Jackson spent the winter at what is now Jackson Hole, WY.

Mountain man Kit Carson began to be known as an overland guide to California.

Millard Fillmore was a member of the New York legislature at this time.

Franklin Pierce was elected to the New Hampshire legislature.

Dover, DE was incorporated as a town.

W.T. Berry became the first postmaster general to be a member of the president's cabinet.

The first post office was constructed in Newport, RI.

The national debt at this time was $58,421,413.67.

science & technology

Peter Cooper built the first practical locomotive in the U.S. It made a 13-mile run in Baltimore in one hour and 12 minutes.

The Delaware & Chesapeake Canal was formally opened.

The first paper-making machine was manufactured in Windham, CT.

The American Fur Co. built Ft. Union at the mouth of the Yellowstone River.

William E. Horner published the first U.S. textbook on pathology (the study of disease).

The first cottonseed oil mill opened in Petersburg, VA.

arts & culture

The first American encyclopedia, the *Encyclopedia Americana*, was published.

Edgar Allan Poe's *Al Araaf, Tamerlane, and Other Poems* was published.

Washington Irving's *The Conquest of Granada* was a best seller this year.

The first U.S. School for the blind opened in Boston.

1830

politics

The population of the 24 states at this time was 12,866,020.

Tampa, FL was established.

Abraham Lincoln moved to Illinois.

Congress enacted the Removal Bill, which resulted in the forced immigration of Indians from the East to the Southwest. This long migration became known as the "Trail of Tears."

The territories of the Sac and Fox Indians (present day WS) were ceded to the U.S.

Chester A. Arthur was born in Fairfield, VT.

Mexico forbade further colonization of Texas by U.S. citizens.

Fur traders William Sublette and David Jackson started from St. Louis through Wyoming, opening the Oregon Trail, for 40 years the most heavily traveled wagon trail in the world.

By this time the U.S. had over 1,200 miles of canals and only 23 miles of railroad track.

President Jackson and Vice President Calhoun had strained relations due to personal conflicts and disagreement on the issue of "nullification," the theory of a state's right to nullify a federal act if it considers it to be unconstitutional.

John Quincy Adams and James K. Polk were both members of Congress at this time.

Millard Fillmore began a law practice in Buffalo, NY.

The U.S. Naval Observatory was established.

A total of 23,322 immigrants arrived in the U.S.

Chicago was laid out at Ft. Dearborn.
The national debt at this time was $48,565,406.00.

science & technology

R.L. Stevens invented T-shaped railroad tracks.

The first railroad station was erected in Baltimore, MD.

Dr. Gideon Lincecum of Mississippi began selling patent medicines in traveling medicine shows.

At this time New Orleans had the largest sugar refinery in the world.

The first sugar beets were grown in Pennsylvania.

religion

Joseph Smith published the *Book of Mormon* in New York and founded the Church of Latter Day Saints.

arts & culture

The banjo was invented by J.W. Sweeeny.

Sarah Hale published "Mary Had a Little Lamb" in *Poems for Children*.

Sod houses began to appear on the prairies.

Cincinnati was called "Porkopolis," because it was the nation's meat-packing center.

Ladies' skirts were shorter and dress sleeves were enormous. Large hats with ribbons and flowers were popular.

1831

politics

The term "Old Glory," to designate the U.S. flag, was first used by William Driver, a New England seaman.

James A. Garfield was born in Ohio.

A total of 22,633 immigrants arrived in the U.S.

The term "abolitionists" was used in reference to those opposing slavery.

A treaty of amity, commerce and navigation was signed with Mexico.

The Black Hawk Indian War and the Sac and Fox Indian War began.

Abraham Lincoln and Jefferson Davis served together under Zachary Taylor in the Sac and Fox Indian War.

The statehouse in North Carolina was destroyed by fire.

Martin Van Buren resigned as secretary of state.

James Monroe died at the age of 73. He was

the third former president to die on July 4.

The failure of the Bank of Maryland caused riots in Baltimore.

The national debt at this time amounted to $39,123,191.68.

science & technology

Cyrus McCormick invented the mechanical reaper.

Chloroform was synthesized by Dr. Samuel Guthrie.

Building and loan associations were opened in Frankford, PA.

The first platform scale was patented.

Guernsey cattle were first imported to Boston at about this time.

J. Henry invented the electric bell.

New York City began using horse-drawn streetcars.

arts & culture

Dr. Samuel Francis Smith composed *America*. He did not know that the tune was the same as that of the British national anthem.

Edgar Allan Poe published his *Poems*.

William Lloyd Garrison began publishing the abolitionist periodical *The Liberator* in Boston.

Jedediah Strong Smith, the well-known explorer and trapper, was killed by Comanche Indians near Santa Fe.

Oranges and lemons, brought to this country by the Spanish, entered American diets at about this time.

The first bank robbery in New York City occurred.

1832

politics

The Democratic Party formally adopted its present name at a convention in Baltimore.

Andrew Jackson became the first presidential candidate nominated at a national convention.

New York Senator Marcy first used the expression, "To the victors belong the spoils."

James Buchanan was named minister to Russia.

H.R. Schoolcraft discovered the source of the Mississippi River.

Both Providence, RI and Wilmington, DE were incorporated.

Abraham Lincoln, at the age of 23, was defeated in his first bid for public office in Illinois.

Vice President Calhoun resigned his office.

Charles Carroll, the last survivor of the signers of the Declaration of Independence, died.

The Chickasaw Indians ceded all their remaining lands east of the Mississippi River to the U.S.

Chief Black Hawk of the Sac and Fox Indians was defeated by the U.S.

Hot Springs National Park in Arkansas was established as a reservation.

science & technology

The first American clipper ship, the *Ann McKim*, was launched at Baltimore.

The American Fur Co. established Fort McKenzie above the mouth of the Marias River.

The first rubber company was established at Roxbury, MA.

The New York and Erie Railroad was chartered.

J. Mathews manufactured the first soda fountain.

Walter Hunt of New York invented the lock stitch sewing machine.

religion

The hymns "Rock of Ages" and "My Faith Looks Up to Thee" were published.

American missionaries took the first general census in Hawaii.

Mormon leader Joseph Smith was tarred and feathered by a mob in Hiram, OH.

arts & culture

Washington Irving wrote *The Alhambra*, a series of stories about the Moors and Spaniards.

More than 4,000 people died in New York in the first cholera epidemic in the U.S.

John Ball taught the first school in the Oregon Territory.

1833

politics

President Jackson was inaugurated for his second term as president. Martin Van Buren was his vice president.

Benjamin Harrison was born in North Bend, OH.

A tax-supported public library was established at Peterborough, NH.

A total of 58,640 immigrants arrived in the U.S.

The Congressional Temperance Society was formed in Washington, DC.

Government funds were removed from U.S. banks by President Jackson.

Dubuque, IA was formed as a settlement named for lead miner Julien Dubuque.

Ft. Dearborn, IL became the incorporated village of Chicago.

John C. Calhoun became a U.S. senator from South Carolina.

Millard Fillmore was elected to the U.S. Congress.

Franklin Pierce was elected to the U.S. Congress.

Bent's Fort, the most important trading post in the Colorado area, was built on the mountain branch of the Santa Fe Trail and the Arkansas River.

Burlington, IA was settled.

The first U.S. Army cavalry unit was formed at Jefferson Barracks, MO.

science & technology

The first steel plow was produced in the U.S. by John Deere.

Samuel Colt began production of the revolver in Paterson, NJ.

The first factory to produce shirts and collars was established in Troy, NY.

religion

Mormon Church leaders were forced to agree to leave Missouri.

Moses Merrill became the first missionary to the Nebraska Indians.

arts & culture

A rudimentary form of baseball was played in Philadelphia by the Olympic Ball Club.

Avocado trees from Mexico were introduced on farms in Florida by H. Perrine.

The first major railroad accident occurred on the Amboy & Bordentown Railroad.

Davy Crockett's autobiography was a best seller this year.

1834

politics

Congress established the Department of Indian Affairs.

The Seminole Indians were ordered to evacuate Florida.

The famous 16 to 1 ratio of silver and gold was authorized by the Second Coinage Act.

A total of 65,365 immigrants arrived in the U.S.

Ft. Hall, the first settlement in Idaho, was founded by N.J. Wyeth.

The Pawnee Expedition began.

Houston, TX and San Francisco, CA were established.

Ft. Laramie, WY was established.

Congress established the Indian Territory.

Abraham Lincoln became a member of the Illinois legislature.

Stephen A. Douglas of Illinois was dubbed the "Little Giant." Douglas debated Abraham Lincoln in 1858.

Stephen Austin was imprisoned for a year by Mexican President Santa Ana.

Brooklyn, NY was chartered as a city.

James Buchanan was elected to the U.S. Senate.

Many tracts and pamphlets began to appear on the abolition of slavery.

The Senate censured President Jackson for removing government deposits from national banks in 1833.

President Jackson made a formal protest to the censure.

President Jackson announced that the national debt would be paid off by January, 1835.

The national debt at this time was $4,760,082.08.

science & technology

An electric motor was constructed by Thomas Davenport.

Cyrus McCormick patented a reaper.

The American Fur Co. was now dominant east the the Continental Divide, while Hudson's Bay Co. was dominant west of the divide.

The first brass kettles were made in Torrington, CT.

The first friction matches were manufactured in Massachusetts.

arts & culture

Until now, tomatoes were thought to be poisonous and were used only as ornaments.

1835

politics

The first attempt to assassinate a president was made on President Jackson at a funeral.

The Liberty Bell cracked while being tolled for the death of Chief Justice John Marshall.

The Texas Rangers were authorized by the Texas provisional povernment.

James K. Polk became the Speaker of the House of Representatives.

The second Seminole War began. It lasted until 1842.

Branch U.S. mints were established at New Orleans, LA, Charlotte, NC and Dahlonega, GA.

Texans first battled with Mexico at Gonzales.

The "Toledo War" erupted over the Michigan-Ohio boundary.

S.T. Mason, 24 years old, was inaugurated as the first governor of Michigan.

A road was opened between Detroit and Chicago.

Andrew Johnson was elected as a state representative of Tennessee.

The Democratic Party was called the Loco Foco party by opponents. "Loco foco" was the name for an early version of the match. The party's name referred to their evening meetings in which they used loco focos to light their lamps.

science & technology

Samuel F.B. Morse invented the telegraph.

The first trains ran between Boston and Providence.

The first mutual life insurance company in the U.S. was chartered.

Samuel Colt applied for a patent on the revolving pistol.

The Boston & Maine Railroad was chartered.

The first successful sugar plantation was organized in Kauai, HI.

The Bowie knife was invented by James Bowie.

The first laundry was opened in Troy, NY.

The first soda water was bottled in Connecticut.

Isaac Fischer of Springfield, VT patented sandpaper.

arts & culture

A two-day fire in New York destroyed 600 warehouses. Losses were estimated at $20 million.

Yacht racing began in Massachusetts.

P.T. Barnum made his first appearance on stage as an assistant to a magician.

James Gordon Bennet published the *New York Herald*, a four-page penny paper.

1836

politics

Arkansas became the twenty-fifth state.

Cleveland, OH was established.

Construction began on the Washington Monument in Washington, DC.

Texas declared itself an independent republic, "the Lone Star Republic." Sam Houston was elected president.

The Alamo at San Antonio, TX was captured by Santa Anna.

Sam Houston defeated Santa Anna at San Jacinto.

The war cry, "Remember the Alamo," was first sounded by Texans at the Battle of San Jacinto.

The U.S. signed a treaty of friendship and commerce with Venezuela.

James Madison died at the age of 85 and was buried at Montpelier, VT.

Aaron Burr, former vice president, died at age 80 in New York.

Stephen F. Austin, known as the Father of Texas, died.

The second Creek Indian War began (1836-1837).

Cherokee disturbances began in the West.

The U.S. Patent Office became a bureau of the State Department.

The Whig Party was organized. Today's Republican Party evolved from Federalists through Whigs into its current form in the early 1850s.

Congress passed the "Gag Resolutions" prohibiting petitions against slavery.

science & technology

The rotary printing press was invented by Richard M. Hoe.

The first safety fuse was manufactured in Simsbury, CT.

The Cumberland Valley Railroad installed sleeping car service, a forerunner of the Pullman cars.

The Western & Atlantic Railroad began operation in Georgia.

Hook and eye fasteners were successfully manufactured in Waterbury, CT.

arts & culture

William H. McGuffey published readers for the public schools. "McGuffey Readers" were standard texts in American schools for nearly a century.

Henry Wadsworth Longfellow was appointed a professor at Harvard.

The *Sandwich Island Gazette* became the first English-language newspaper in Hawaii.

1837

politics

Martin Van Buren was inaugurated as the eighth president. Richard M. Johnson was his vice president.

Michigan was admitted as the twenty-sixth state.

A total of 79,340 immigrants arrived in the U.S.

Grover Cleveland was born in Caldwell, NJ.

Congress increased the number of Supreme Court justices from seven to nine.

Toledo, OH, Little Rock, AR and Galveston, TX were established.

Franklin Pierce was elected to the Senate from New Hampshire.

Many U.S. citizens joined the "Patriot War" in Canada.

The Secretary of State ordered the arrest of American citizens giving aid to the Canadian Rebellion.

Chicago, IL, with a population of 3,297, was incorporated as a city.

The first State Board of Education was founded in Massachusetts.

The Seminole Indians were defeated by General Zachary Taylor in Florida.

The U.S. recognized Texas as an independent republic.

The Osage Indian conflict began.

science & technology

The first locomotive steam whistle was used.

The first brass clock works were invented in Bristol, CT.

The first threshing machine to use steam was patented.

Anthracite coal was first used in smelting iron in Pennsylvania.

Samuel Morse demonstrated his telegraph machine to Congress.

Charles Goodyear received the first rubber patent.

arts & culture

The Pickwick Papers became the first of Charles Dickens' works to be published in America.

Nathaniel Hawthorne's *Twice-Told Tales* was a best seller this year.

The first magazine for the blind was published in Philadelphia. It used raised type.

Music instruction in public schools began in Boston.

The first state school for the blind opened in Columbus, OH.

A smallpox epidemic raged among Indians in the northern Great Plains.

1838

politics

The Iowa Territory was formed from the Wisconsin Territory.

John Quincy Adams presented petitions to Congress opposing slavery and the annexation of Texas.

Texas withdrew its annexation request.

The remaining Cherokee Indians in Georgia were forceably ejected by federal troops and moved to Indian Territory.

The International Copyright Act was passed by Congress.

Frontier disturbances occurred between New York and Canada.

General Zachary Taylor was named commanding officer of all Florida forces.

Thirty-six settlers in Willamette Valley, OR signed a petition asking the U.S. to take possession of Oregon.

Navy Lieutenant Charles Wilkes made his Antarctic expedition.

The first silver mine was discovered in Lexington, NC.

John Tyler was elected to the Virginia House of Delegates.

Between 1838 and 1863, the Corps of Topographical Engineers of the U.S. Army made extensive maps of the American West.

The Aroostook Indian disturbances began.

All railroads in the U.S. were designated as postal routes by Congress.

science & technology

The first transatlantic steamship service began.

Manila paper was created in South Braintree, MA.

The first tool factory was established in Nashua, NH.

The Puget Sound Agricultural Company was formed.

The Wabash Railroad began.

B. Sheridon built the first embossing press in New York City.

religion

The Christmas hymn "Joy To The World" was published.

The first Catholic missionaries arrived in Oregon.

arts & culture

The first music convention was held in Boston.

A large fire in Charleston, SC destroyed 1,158 buildings.

The *New York Herald* became the first U.S. newspaper to employ European correspondents.

1839

politics

Congress passed an act prohibiting dueling in Washington, DC. (1839 cont.)
A total of 68,069 immigrants arrived in the U.S.

James K. Polk was elected Governor of Tennessee.

Between 1839 and 1859, corn production in the U.S. increased from 327 to 838 million bushels. Wheat production increased from 84 to 173 million bushels.

Chattanooga, TN was established.

China trade and whaling activities led many U.S. Ships to Samoa.

Ulysses S. Grant entered West Point.

Captain John A. Sutter, on his way to Sitka, AK became stranded in California and built a fort near Sacramento in 1841.

France became the first European nation to recognize the independence of Texas.

The Aroostook War was fought over the boundary between Maine and the British provinces.

The first state military school was established at Lexington, VA.

Springfield was made the capital of Illinois.

The national debt at this time was 10.434,221.14.

science & technology

The first electric powered printing press was used in New York.

The first express service between New York and Boston began.

North Carolina chartered the first silver mining concern in the U.S.

Charles Goodyear made the first vulcanized rubber.

religion

More than 12,000 Mormons were driven out of Missouri.

The first edition of the Bible in Hawaiian was printed.

arts & culture

Edgar Allen Poe wrote *The Fall of the House of Usher*.

Henry Wadsworth Longfellow published his first book of verse, *Voices of the Night*.

A smallpox epidem,ic in Russian America (now Alaska) caused many deaths.

The game of baseball was invented by Abner Doubleday in Cooperstown, (1839 cont.)
NY. Doubleday's plan of bases has never been changed.

Photography began to be practiced in America.

1840

politics

The population of the twenty-six states at this time was 17,069,453.

There were 2,818 miles of railroad track in the U.S. at this time.

The U.S. expedition led by Captain Charles Wilkes laid claim to the continent of Antarctica for the U.S.

Texas signed a treaty with Great Britain.

General Zachary Taylor commanded a division at Baton Rouge, LA.

The U.S. signed a treaty of commerce with Portugal.

American's had not yet settled one-third of the states.

The Oregon Trail became an immigrant's road.

The Battle of the Everglades was fought with the Florida Indians.

Congress appropriated $25,000 to establish Maine, New Hampshire and British Provinces boundary lines.

North Carolina's new capital at Raleigh was finished.

"Tippecanoe and Tyler, Too" became the campaign slogan for William Henry Harrison and John Tyler in their bid for the presidency and vice presidency.

President Van Buren established a 10-hour work day for federal employees.

science & technology

The American Society of Dental Surgeons was founded in Baltimore.

The first dental college opened in Baltimore.

Until 1840, nearly all hay corps in the U.S. were still being harvested with scythes.

The Census showed 57,565 retail stores in the U.S.

John William Draper took the first photograph of the moon.

The Pennsylvania & Ohio Canal opened.

arts & culture

The most popular books of the time were *Two Years Before the Mast* and *The Pathfinder*.

The first use of the expression "OK" referred to Old Kinderhook, Van Buren's birthplace.

The first bowling tournament was held in New York City.

In these days ladies used special post office windows so as to avoid tobacco-chewing men.

1841

politics

William Henry Harrison was inaugurated as the ninth president. John Tyler was his vice president.

One month after his inauguration, President Harrison died at the age of 68. John Tyler thus became the first vice president to become president after the president's death.

The uniform bankruptcy system was made law by Congress.

Manjiro Nakahama became the first Japanese immigrant to the U.S.

The first covered wagon arrived in California via the Oregon Trail.

A total of 80,289 immigrants arrived in the U.S.

A political feud kept Tennessee from having a U.S. senator from 1841 to 1843.

Alabama introduced the licensing of dentists.

During the 1840s and 1850s, many Irish immigrants arrived in the U.S. because of the potato blight in Ireland. Many Germans arrived because of political conditions in Germany.

The pre-emption law was passed by Congress, giving squatters rights. This law was repealed in 1891.

General Zachary Taylor became known as "Old Rough and Ready" during the Seminole War.

By now the U.S. had over 3,000 miles of canals.

All of President Tyler's cabinet resigned except Daniel Webster.

The national debt at this time was $5,250,875.54.

science & technology

Samuel M. Kier made the first commercial use of oil in the U.S.

The first credit information agency was begun in New York.

Cornstarch was patented.

The first life preserver was patented in New York. It was made of cork.

New York City tested the first fire engine.

The first typesetting machine was patented.

arts & culture

Edgar Allan Poe's first detective story, "The Murders in the Rue Morgue," was published in *Graham's Magazine*.

James Fenimore Cooper wrote *The Deerslayer*.

The *New York Tribune* was founded by Horace Greeley.

The first annual state fair was held in Syracuse, NY.

The steamer *President* was lost in a storm en route from Liverpool to the U.S. with 136 people aboard.

1842

politics

Henry Clay resigned from Congress after 40 years of public service.

The Reapportionment Act was passed by Congress. This established that congressmen would be elected by districts.

A total of 104,565 immigrants arrived in the U.S.

Colonel J.C. Fremont began the first exploring expedition of the Rocky Mountains. He hired Kit Carson as a guide.

The U.S.-Great Britain treaty settled the Maine boundary.

The Seminole War ended in Florida.

The fiscal year beginning was changed from January 1 to July 1.

Ft. Scott, KS began as a post between Ft. Leavenworth and Ft. Gibson.

Connecticut adopted the motto "Sustinet Qui Transtulit" ("He who is transplanted still sustains").

The second Wilkes Expedition proved that Antarctica is a continent.

The national debt at this time was $13,594,480.73.

science & technology

The first commercial artificial fertilizer was produced by John B. Lawes.

The first patent for a sewing machine was granted to J.J. Greenough.

Ether was first used in a surgical operation at Jefferson, GA.

Adobe Ft. El Pueblo (now Pueblo, CO) was built by fur traders.

Copper mining began near Keewenaw Point, MI.

arts & culture

Edgar Allan Poe published "The Masque of the Read Death."

The New York Philharmonic Society was founded.

E.P. Christy organized The Christy Minstrels.

Charles Dickens visited the U.S.

P.T. Barnum opened the American Museum in New York City.

President Tyler's wife Letitia died in the White House.

The first business school opened in Rochester, NY.

Influenza (called the grippe) was prevalent throughout the U.S.

1843

politics

More than 1,000 settlers left Independence, MO on their way to Oregon.

The president of Mexico warned the U.S. not to annex Texas.

William McKinley was born in Niles, OH.

The U.S. sent its first diplomatic representative to the Hawaiian Islands.

A total of 52,496 immigrants arrived in the U.S.

Colonel J.C. Fremont explored from Salt Lake to the mouth of the Columbia River.

Rumors circulated that the British planned to occupy Oregon.

The clipper ship era in America lasted from about 1843 to 1868.

England and France recognized Hawaii's independence.

The Department of the Interior was formed.

The Bunker Hill monument in Boston was dedicated by Daniel Webster.

Influenza epidemics were sometimes called "Tyler grip" in reference to the unpopular president.

Andrew Johnson was elected to the U.S. House of Representatives.

A truce was declared between Mexico and Texas.

science & technology

Congress granted Samuel Morse $30,000.00 to hang electric wire between Washington, DC and Baltimore for a telegraph service.

B.T. Babbitt introduced soap powder at about this time.

Samuel Colt, the inventor of the revolver, laid the first submarine cable in New York Harbor.

The first egg incubator was patented by N.E. Guerin.

religion

The B'nai Brith, a Jewish organization, was founded in New York.

arts & culture

The songs "I Dreamt I Dwelt in Marble Halls" and "Columbia, the Gem of the Ocean" were popular at this time.

Francis Scott Key died in Maryland.

Noah Webster died in Connecticut.

The first matinee performance opened at the Olympic Theater in New York City.

1844

politics

President John Tyler married in New York City, thus becoming the first president to marry while in office.

A total of 78,615 immigrants arrived in the U.S.

James K. Polk became the first "dark horse" candidate for U.S. president.

A treaty of peace, amity and commerce was signed with China.

A treaty for admission of Texas into the Union was signed.

The national debt at this time was $23,461,652.00.

science & technology

The first telegraph message sent by Samuel Morse was, "What hath God wrought?"

The Niagara suspension bridges were proposed.

The steamboat *J.M. White* steamed from New Orleans to St. Louis in a record three days and 23 hours.

Iron ore was discovered in the Michigan Upper Peninsula.

The first stained glass was installed in Pelham Manor, NY.

Stuart Perry patented the first gas engine in New York.

The first steam heating was installed in Boston.

The first iron railroad tracks were laid.

The first telegraph station opened in Washington, DC.

Charles Goodyear patented rubber vulcanizing.

religion

Joseph Smith, the founder of the Mormon Church, and his brother were murdered in Illinois.

Brigham Young was elected president of the Mormon Church.

The first Seventh Day Adventist Church opened in Washington Center, NH.

arts & culture

The polka dance was introduced and quickly became quite popular in America.

The first bridal suite and the first private bath in a hotel were introduced in New York.

The New York Yacht Club was organized.

1845

politics

James K. Polk was inaugurated as the eleventh president. George M. Dallas was his vice president.

Florida was admitted as the twenty-seventh state.

Texas became the twenty-eighth state.

The U.S. Naval Academy officially opened at Annapolis, MD.

A total of 114,371 immigrants arrived in the U.S.

Mexico declared war against the U.S.

A treaty of commerce was completed with Belgium.

The concept of "manifest destiny" was used in support of annexing Texas.

J. Buchanan was named Secretary of State.

Congress overrode a presidential veto for the first time.

Marine Lt. I.W. Curtis called attention to the importance of Pearl Harbor in the defense of Hawaii.

President Polk reaffirmed the Monroe Doctrine.

Explorer John C. Fremont became known as The Pathfinder.

President Polk's wife Sarah prohibited liquor and dancing in the White House.

Andrew Jackson died at the age of 78 in Tennessee.

U.S. postage stamps were authorized.

The national debt at this time was $15,925,303.00.

science & technology

The first oilcloth factory was established in Winthrop, ME.

The first advertising calendar was published by an Auburn, NY insurance company.

religion

The Southern Baptist Convention and the Methodist Episcopal Church were both established.

arts & culture

Edgar Allan Poe published *The Raven and Other Poems*.

Leonora, an American opera by W.H. Fry, was produced in Philadelphia.

German actors began putting on plays in New York beer halls.

A.J. Cartwright of the Knickerbocker Club devised the first formal rules for playing baseball.

Texas longhorn cattle began to be well known at about this time.

The *National Police Gazette* was first published.

Fires destroyed 1,000 buildings in New York City and 1,000 buildings in Pittsburgh.

1846

politics

Iowa was admitted as the twenty-ninth state.

The U.S. declared war on Mexico.

Congress authorized building of the Smithsonian Institution upon the bequest of James Smithson.

Abraham Lincoln was elected to the U.S. House of Representatives.

The "Bear Flag Revolt" began in California.

The Oregon Treaty was signed, establishing the boundary between the U.S. and British northwest territories at the forty-ninth parallel.

Commodore Stockton took possession of Los Angeles. Later it fell again to Mexican forces.

Commodore Perry's forces bombarded Tabasco, Mexico.

Commodore David Conner captured Tampico on the Gulf Coast of Mexico.

The Donner party, a group of emigrants traveling from Illinois to California, was stranded for the winter at Truckee Lake, where many of them engaged in cannibalism and perished.

St. Paul, MN was settled by Americans.

Florida adopted the motto, "In God We Trust."

A total of 154,416 immigrants arrived in the U.S.

The large Irish immigration to the U.S. continued due to the potato famine.

General Kearney annexed New Mexico for the U.S.

The national debt was $15,550,202.00.

science & technology

The first gingham factory in the U.S. was founded in Clinton, MA.

The first rotary printing press was used in Philadelphia.

The first artificial leg was patented in Meredith, NH.

The first baking soda was manufactured in New York City.

The Pennsylvania Railroad was chartered

religion

Brigham Young led a wagon train of Mormons westward from Illinois.

arts & culture

Herman Melville published *Typee*.

Henry Wadsworth Longfellow wrote *The Belfry of Bruges*.

The first tattoo shop opened in New York.

The first recorded baseball game in history was played in Hoboken, NJ.

1847

politics

General Winfield Scott commanded the first large-scale amphibious operation in U.S. military history in Vera Cruz, Mexico.

The Smithsonian Institution was formally dedicated in Washington, DC.

General Scott led U.S. troops into Mexico City. U.S. Marines began their guard of the "Halls of Montezuma."

California was declared a U.S. territory.

Jefferson Davis was elected to the Senate from Mississippi.

Atlanta, GA was established.

Council Grove, KS was established as the final jumping-off point for settlers on their way to Santa Fe.

A total of 234,968 immigrants arrived in the U.S.

New Hampshire became the first state to legalize a 10-hour working day.

Franklin Pierce was a brigadier general during the Mexican War.

Captain Robert E. Lee, Lieutenant George B. McClellan and Lieutenant Pierre G.T. Beauregard all served on General Scott's staff during the Mexican War.

Michigan abolished capital punishment.

Congress provided for gas lighting of the Capitol Building and its grounds.

The national debt at this time was $38,826,534.00.

science & technology

Thomas Edison was born.

The American Medical Association was organized in Philadelphia.

The first issue of adhesive postage stamps was made in the U.S.

The Chicago & Rock Island Railroad was incorporated.

The first rubber tire was patented.

The American Fur Co. established Ft. Benton, MT.

The first telephone connection was made between New York and Boston.

religion

The first Mormon emigrants arrived in Utah and established Salt Lake City.

arts & culture

The Astor Place Opera House opened in New York City.

Chicago's first theater was erected by J.B. Rice.

1848

politics

science & technology

religion

arts & culture

politics

Wisconsin became the thirtieth state.

Gold was discovered in California.

The war with Mexico ended, and all lands north of the Gila River were ceded to the U.S.

President Polk offered to buy Cuba from Spain for $100 million.

The first Chinese immigrants reached San Francisco at about this time. By 1852, approximately 18,000 Chinese had arrived in the U.S.

A total of 226,527 immigrants arrived in the U.S.

The first U.S. whaling ship entered the Arctic Ocean through the Bering Strait.

Congress approved the Oregon Territorial Government.

The Rio Grande River was established as the southern boundary of Texas.

science & technology

The first ice cream freezer was patented in Baltimore.

The Chicago Board of Trade was formed.

The first dental chair was patented in Syracuse, NY.

The first canned sweet corn was sold in Portland, ME.

The first chewing gum was manufactured in Bangor, ME.

The first macaroni factory was established in Brooklyn, NY.

The Chicago & North Western Railroad was chartered.

The first baby carriage was manufactured in New York City.

religion

Spiritualism was becoming popular in the U.S.

arts & culture

The fairy tales of Hans Christian Anderson were first published in the U.S.

Stephen Collins Foster's song "Oh! Susanna" was published.

The play *Monte Cristo* was introduced in New York City.

The first school for the mentally handicapped opened in Massachusetts.

A footbridge was completed over the Niagara Gorge.

A New York newspaper group organized the Associated Press.

1849

politics

Zachary Taylor was inaugurated as the twelfth president. Millard Fillmore was his vice president.

Hundreds perished in the Gold Rush to California.

A total of 297,024 immigrants arrived in the U.S.

The Apache, Navajo and Utah Indian Wars began. These lasted until 1861.

Congress approved a territorial government for Minnesota.

James K. Polk died at the age of 53 and was buried in Nashville, TN.

Death Valley, CA was named by the Manly-Hunt party. Many members of the party perished there.

There were now 9,000 miles of railroad track in the U.S.

The U.S. Patent Office was transferred from the State Department to the Interior Department.

Private mints sprang up to coin gold as government money became scarce.

The California Constitution was ratified by voters.

The national debt at this time was $63,061,858.00.

science & technology

Walter Hunt patented the safety pin.

The Smithsonian Institution first published weather forecasts.

Elizabeth Blackwell of Geneva, NY became the first woman physician in the world.

One of the first coal mining labor organizations was formed.

Stagecoach service was now provided between Independence, MO and Santa Fe, NM.

The wire gauge was developed and silk thread on spools was patented.

The gas mask, the envelope machine and the rock drill were patented.

arts & culture

Edgar Allan Poe died at the age of 40.

The saxophone, invented by Adolphe Sax, was introduced to New York audiences.

Over 400 buildings and 27 steamships were destroyed in a St. Louis fire.

Twenty people were killed in a riot at the Astor Place Opera House in New York City.

Ladies now puffed their hair over a cushion atop the head.

1850

politics

California became the thirty-first state.

The population of the 31 states at this time was 23,191,876.

President Zachary Taylor died in office at the age of 66. Millard Fillmore became the thirteenth president.

San Francisco, CA had 34,776 residents at this time. In 1840, only 500 people had lived in the city.

Sailors on 50 ships deserted in San Francisco to search for gold.

The creation of Central Park was proposed in New York City.

Utah and New Mexico were made U.S. territories.

Kansas City, MO was established.

Daniel Webster was named Secretary of State.

A total of 369,986 immigrants arrived in the U.S.

The estimated national wealth of the U.S. was $7,135,780.00.

Arizona was made part of the New Mexico territory by Congress.

Sacramento, CA was established.

From January 1 to July 8, 42,000 emigrants and 9,720 wagons passed through Laramie, WY on their way to the gold mines of California.

Gold was discovered near Denver, CO.

science & technology

The first agricultural binder in the U.S. was invented by John E. Heath.

The Southern Pacific Railroad was chartered.

The Studebaker Blacksmith Shop in California produced wheelbarrows for miners.

The Armour Butcher Shop opened in California to supply miners with meat.

The famous clipper ship the *Flying Cloud* was built at East Boston, MA.

The roll-top desk was invented.

The New York Produce Exchange was formed.

The first derby hat, eight-day clock, and cork were manufactured.

arts & culture

Nathaniel Hawthorne's *The Scarlet Letter* was published.

Jenny Lind, the "Swedish Nightingale," gave her first American performance in New York.

Harper's Magazine was founded in New York.

Female clerks were hired for the first time by stores in Philadelphia.

Whist and Faro were popular gambling games at this time.

1851

politics

science & technology

arts & culture

The city of Portland, OR was established.

Yosemite Valley in California was discovered.

About 250,000 Indians roamed the western half of the U.S. at this time.

California vigilance committees were formed at this time to stop lawlessness.

America's first international rail connection linked Montreal and Boston.

A fire in the Congressional Library in Washington, DC destroyed 35,000 of the 55,000 volumes it contained.

The first permanent white settlement in Colorado was established at San Luis.

The Oregon and Washington Indian Wars began and lasted until 1856.

Isaac Merrit Singer patented the sewing machine.

The first artificial eyes were manufactured.

The Illinois Central and Missouri Pacific Railroads were chartered.

The first condensed milk was produced by Gail Borden in Brooklyn.

Stephen Foster composed "The Old Folks at Home."

Uncle Tom's Cabin appeared serially in newspapers.

The House of Seven Gables by Nathaniel Hawthorne was published.

Herman Melville's *Moby Dick* was published.

San Francisco audiences saw their first performance of an Italian opera.

The first American Y.M.C.A. opened in Boston.

The phrase, "Go west, young man, go west," was first used by John B. Soule, the editor of the *Terre Haute Express.*

The bloomer dress was introduced in Seneca Falls, NY by Elizabeth Miller and was popularized by Amelia Bloomer.

The losses from two fires in San Francisco amounted to over $6.5 million.

Most city streets and some downtown streets in New York City were still unpaved at this time.

The *New York Times* began publication.

Ladies' soft felt hats were introduced in New York City.

The first baseball uniforms were worn by the New York Knickerbockers.

1852

politics

Marcy's Exploring Expedition set out to find the source of the Red River.

A total of 371,603 immigrants arrived in the U.S.

Commodore M.C. Perry, the brother of O.H. Perry, set off on a trade expedition to Japan.

In California, whites killed at least 50,000 Indians between 1849 and 1852.

The first Chinese contract laborers arrived in Hawaii.

The U.S. established a second mint in San Francisco.

Henry Clay, former U.S. statesman, died at the age of 75.

Secretary of State Daniel Webster died at the age of 70.

Massachusetts was the first state to enact a compulsory school attendance law.

Ohio was the first state to enact the 10-hour work day for women.

The U.S. first authorized stamped envelopes.

Ft. Yuma, AZ was established.

science & technology

The first horse blankets were manufactured.

The first use of the word "telegram" appeared in the *Albany Evening Journal*.

The American Pharmaceutical Association was founded in Philadelphia.

Alexander B. Latta invented the first effective fire engine.

E.G. Otis invented the elevator, making skyscrapers possible.

Wells, Fargo & Co. was organized for express service in western America.

The first bright leaf tobacco was produced in North Carolina.

Direct railroad service began between New York and Chicago.

arts & culture

Harriet Beecher Stowe's book *Uncle Tom's Cabin* was published in Boston.

Nathaniel Hawthorne published *A Wonder Book*, a collection of tales for children.

The first public bath-house was built in New York.

W. Phillips wrote the famous words, "Eternal vigilance is the price of liberty."

The American Geographical Society was founded in New York City.

The first major stagecoach robbery was staged by the Williams Gang in California. They made off with $7,500.00.

1853

politics

Franklin Pierce was inaugurated as the fourteenth president. William R. King was his vice president.

The U.S. negotiated the Gadsden Purchase with Mexico for $10 million, settling the U.S.-Mexican border dispute.

Andrew Johnson was elected Governor of Tennessee.

The Territory of Washington was formed.

Commodore M.C. Perry of the U.S. Navy opened trade with Japan.

A total of 386,645 immigrants arrived in the U.S.

The first assay office opened in New York for evaluating metals.

Steven's survey was sponsored by the Federal Government to find a route for a railway line to the Pacific.

The first U.S. warship, the *Dreadnaught*, was launched from Newburyport, MA.

The S.S. *Akamsai*, the first inter-island steamer, arrived in Hawaii.

The national debt at this time was $59,803,117.00.

science & technology

The New York Clearinghouse was the first in the U.S. to handle the checks of banks.

H.E. Steinway & Sons opened their company to manufacture pianos in New York.

The first plate glass was manufactured in Cheshire, MA.

arts & culture

Nathaniel Hawthorne's *Tanglewood Tales* was published.

L.W. Mason & G.A. Veazie began publishing music books and charts.

Stephen Foster wrote "My Old Kentucky Home" and "Old Dog Tray."

The first newspaper story on baseball appeared in the *New York Mercury*.

A yellow fever epidemic killed more than 5,000 people in New Orleans.

The steamer *San Francisco*, bound for California, sank with 250 soldiers aboard. All 250 perished.

The first state fair in North Carolina was held in Raleigh.

The Delevan House in Albany, NY was the first hotel to employ waitresses.

The first fire department to be paid a salary was established in Cincinnati, OH.

1854

politics

The Republican Party was formed at Jackson, MI and Ripon, WI.

The first land office opened in Kansas.

Kansas was organized as a territory.

A total of 427,833 immigrants arrived in the U.S.

Congress approved a system of private bonded warehouses.

The first federal court held session in the Washington Territory. The first legislature in the territory also opened.

A public school system was established in Texas.

The Comanche Indian War ended.

J.M. Langston, a Negro emancipated from slavery, became the first black admitted to the Ohio Bar.

St. Paul, MN was established.

Topeka, Lawrence, Leavenworth and Atchison, KS were all established.

In a speech in Peoria, IL Abraham Lincoln called for the gradual emancipation of the slaves.

science & technology

Walter Hunt invented the paper collar.

The first fireproof building in the U.S. was built in New York.

The first copper mine opened in Ajo, AZ.

James Oliver of Indiana invented the iron plow.

The first street-cleaning machine was used in Philadelphia.

A.H. Allen of Boston patented the folding theater chair.

Wood pulp and rag paper were first manufactured in Troy, NY.

arts & culture

Stephen Foster wrote "Jeannie with the Light Brown Hair."

Maria S. Cummins wrote *The Lamplighter*.

The accordian was patented.

The Nebraska Palladium was the first newspaper published in the Nebraska Territory.

The *Kansas Weekly Herald* was the first newspaper published in Kansas.

P.T. Barnum took his circus on a tour of Europe.

The first baby show was held in Springfield, OH.

Alfalfa was introduced in California.

Hoopskirts with steel wires and tape were added to ladies' wardrobes.

1855

politics

Kansas elected its first territorial legislature.

The first Pacific Coast lighthouse was built at Point Loma in San Diego, CA.

A total of 200,877 immigrants arrived in the U.S.

U.S. citizenship for Americans born abroad was approved by Congress.

The war with the Apache, Navajo and Utah Indians ended.

The Snake Indian Expedition and the Yakima Expedition set off to explore the Washington Territory.

The 1855-1856 Cheyenne and Arapaho Indian conflict began.

The U.S. Cavalry was greatly increased to counter the Indian warfare.

The Federal Court of Claims was created by Congress to pay the debts of the U.S.

The Yakima Indian Wars were fought in the Pacific Northwest.

The first postal directory was published in Washington, DC.

The national debt at this time was $35,586,956.00

science & technology

Kerosene oil from bituminous shale was patented.

The Pennsylvania Rock Oil Co. was the first oil business in the U.S.

Henry Bessemer patented the steel-making process.

Marble soda fountains were manufactured in Boston.

A railroad bridge was completed over the Niagara Gorge.

The annual value of farm equipment produced in the U.S. during the 1850s rose from $152 million to $246 million.

Gold was first used for filling dental cavities.

The Western Union Telegraph Company was founded.

I.M. Singer patented the first sewing machine motor.

arts & culture

Walt Whitman's *Leaves of Grass* was published.

Henry Wadsworth Longfellow published his "The Song of Hiawatha."

Alice Hawthorne published "Listen to the Mocking Bird."

Washington Irving coined the expression "the almighty dollar."

The expression "king cotton" came from the book *Cotton Is King* by D. Christy.

The Barter Gang robbed a Wells Fargo stagecoach of $80,000 in California.

1856

politics

Woodrow Wilson was born in Staunton, VA.

Abraham Lincoln became known at the Illinois Republican state convention.

The Copyright Law was passed by Congress.

The first Republican Party national convention was held in Philadelphia.

The Seminole Indian War began.

The governor proclaimed the Territory of Kansas in a state of insurrection.

The Battle of Black Jack was the first engagement in the Kansas Border War.

"Free soil, free speech, free men, and Fremont," was the Republican campaign slogan in the Fremont presidential campaign.

John Brown, abolitionist who believed in taking direct action to end slavery, killed five pro-slavery adherants in Kansas.

Several uninhabited atolls in the Pacific were claimed by the U.S. in the 1850s.

Lawyer turned soldier-of-fortune, William Walker, landed in Nicaragua with a small party and proclaimed himself president. He was expelled the next year.

The American flag was first raised in Japan.

Seattle was attacked by Indians and martial law was declared in Puget Sound.

The S.S. *Decatur* repulsed Indians attacking Seattle.

Lieutenant P.H. Sheridan helped to bring relief to settlers on the Columbia River.

Massachusetts authorized the first state fish commission.

Treaties of friendship and commerce were completed with Siam and Persia.

science & technology

The first blotting paper was manufactured in New Haven, CT.

The first railroad bridge over the Mississippi River connected Rock Island, IL and Davenport, IA.

The Illinois Central Railroad was completed.

Borax was discovered at Tuscan Springs, CA.

The first railroad in California was built.

The North Carolina Railroad was completed from Goldsboro to Charlotte.

Charles E. Barnes patented the first machine gun.

arts & culture

The song "Jingle Bells" was published.

The opera, *La Traviata*, received its American premiere in New York City.

Whittier published his poem "The Barefoot Boy."

1857

politics

James Buchanan was inaugurated as the fifteenth president. J.C. Breckinridge was his vice president.

William H. Taft was born in Cincinnati, OH.

Congress declared that foreign coins were no longer legal tender in the U.S.

Gold was discovered in the Rocky Mountains.

Sioux City, IA was established.

The Civil War in Kansas ended.

A total of 246,945 immigrants arrived in the U.S.

President Buchanan removed Brigham Young from his post as governor of the Utah Territory.

Nickel coins were authorized by Congress.

Oregon adopted the motto, "The union."

Benjamin Harrison was the City Attorney of Indianapolis, IN.

A meeting of the unemployed in Philadelphia drew 10,000.

At this time, 10% of Americans were of foreign birth.

The Sioux Indian troubles began in Minnesota and Iowa.

The Mountain Meadow Massacre occurred in Utah.

Andrew Johnson was elected to the Senate.

science & technology

The first patent was granted for a post-marking and stamp-cancelling machine.

A patent for the process of converting pig iron to steel was awarded to W. Kelley.

The first attempt to lay an Atlantic cable failed.

W.W. Chandler insulated the first boxcar for shipping meats and dairy products.

Stagecoach service was established between San Antonio and San Diego, a 1,475-mile route.

The first oil lamp was developed.

The first toilet paper was manufactured in New York City.

The first electric fire alarm was patented.

arts & culture

The magazine *Atlantic Monthly* began publication.

Central Park was laid out in New York City.

The first baseball association was formed, and new rules fixed the length of the game at nine innings.

1858

politics

Minnesota became the thirty-second state.

Theodore Roosevelt was born in New York City.

Gold was found in Arizona.

The phrase "Pike's Peak or bust" was adopted by gold-rushers heading for Colorado.

A total of 119,501 immigrants arrived in the U.S.

The slave ship *Echo* was captured at the Charleston harbor, and 300 slaves were returned to Liberia.

The first overland mail from San Francisco reached St. Louis.

The famous Lincoln-Douglas debates took place in Illinois.

The Mohave Indians along the Colorado River were subdued.

By now the U.S. had nearly 30,000 miles of railroad track.

John Butterfield & Associates began the Southern Overland Mail stagecoach route from Missouri to California.

Boston erected the first street mailboxes for letters.

Two California miners found gold at Goldcreek, MT.

Joseph Heco became the first Japanese National to be granted U.S. citizenship.

The national debt at this time amounted to $44,911,881.00.

science & technology

Richard Esterbrook developed the first successful steel ink pens.

The first cable message was sent across the Atlantic Ocean. After the first message, the cable broke.

The first burglar alarm was installed.

G.M. Pullman remodeled two railroad cars into sleeping cars.

H.L. Lipman patented the first pencil with an attached eraser.

arts & culture

Henry Wadsworth Longfellow wrote "The Courtship of Miles Standish."

The Y.W.C.A. was organized.

The National Association of Baseball Players was organized. It included 16 New York clubs.

The first National Billiard Championship was held in Detroit.

1859

politics

Oregon was admitted as the thirty-third state.

The first major silver strike in America was made in Nevada.

John Brown seized the arsenal at Harper's Ferry, VA. He was later convicted and hanged.

A total of 188,616 immigrants arrived in the U.S.

Denver, CO was established.

At this time there were fifteen slave states south of the Mason-Dixon line.

At this time most of the population west of the Rocky Mountains was in Oregon.

New York established the first state insurance department.

The national debt at this time was $58,496,837.00.

science & technology

E.L. Drake drilled the first successful oil well in the U.S. in Pennsylvania.

Pullman's first sleeping car made its first run.

The Atchison & Topeka Railroad was chartered. Later the name was changed to the Atchison, Topeka & the Santa Fe.

The first paper bag manufacturing machine was patented in Clinton, MA.

Charles Darwin's book on evolution, *The Origin of the Species*, was published.

G.B. Simpson invented the first electric range in Washington, DC.

Chicago introduced its first horse-drawn streetcars.

The Fifth Avenue Hotel in New York City was the first hotel with an elevator.

By now 1.3 million Americans were working in factories and industries.

arts & culture

Dan Emmett composed the song "Dixie."

Novelist Washington Irving died at the age of 76.

The first newspaper in South Dakota, *The Democrat*, was published.

The Rocky Mountain News was the first newspaper in Colorado.

The Blind School in St. Louis adopted the Braille system.

1860

politics

The population of the 33 states at this time was 31,443,321.

The Pony Express was established between St. Joseph, MO and Sacramento, CA. The route was 1,980 miles long and used 80 riders and 420 horses. The riders changed horses every 10 miles at 190 stations.

Congress enacted a bill establishing the Government Printing Office.

A total of 150,237 immigrants arrived in the U.S.

The estimated national wealth at this time was $16,159,616,000.00.

The Union Army was composed of 16,435 men at this time.

General John Pershing was born.

It was estimated that 20,000 wagons were in use on the Great Plains.

The U.S. Census showed that of a white population of 8,039,000, there were 383,637 people in the 15 slaveholding states owned slaves.

South Carolina became the first state to secede from the Union.

science & technology

The corkscrew was patented in New York.

The first repeating rifle in the U.S. was produced by Oliver F. Winchester.

Darwin's *Origin of the Species* first appeared in America.

The first commercial oil refinery was established in Oil Creek Valley, PA.

Ironclad steamships were introduced.

U.S. cotton plantations exported 5 million bales of cotton.

The first aerial photo in America was taken of Boston from a balloon.

religion

The first permanent settlement in Idaho was established by Mormons.

arts & culture

Stephen Foster published "Old Black Joe."

Randall wrote "Maryland, My Maryland," and set it to the tune of an old drinking song.

The game of croquet was introduced in the U.S. from England.

Men began wearing knickers for sports.

A bartender at a hotel in San Francisco concocted the first dry martini.

1861

politics

Abraham Lincoln was inaugurated as the sixteenth president. Hannibal Hamlin was his vice president.

Kansas became the thirty-fourth state.

Mississippi, Florida, Alabama, Georgia, Louisiana, Texas, Virginia, Arkansas, North Carolina and Tennessee seceded from the Union.

The Confederate States of America were formed at Montgomery, AL. Jefferson Davis was inaugurated as their president.

The Confederate convention adopted the Confederate flag, and later changed it.

The Nevada and Dakota Territories were formed with the division of the Territory of Utah.

The Confederate Congress adopted a constitution and enacted a coinage bill.

The Civil War began at Ft. Sumpter, SC.

The capital of the Confederate State was moved from Montgomery, AL to Richmond, VA.

The first casualties of the Civil War came at Baltimore, MD.

The Choctaw Indians declared their allegiance to the Confederate States.

President Lincoln called for 42,000 volunteers for the Union Army and Navy.

Congress passed the first income tax law to aid in financing the Civil War.

Congress authorized the Medal of Honor for valor.

The U.S. Army had 186,751 men at this time.

The Battle of Belmont, MO was General Ulysses S. Grant's first Civil War battle and his first defeat.

In Arizona and New Mexico, the 1861-1890

Apache Indian War began.

A territorial government was established in Colorado.

President Lincoln suspended all commerce with the seceded states.

Charleston, New Orleans, Mobile and Savannah were all blockaded.

The national debt at this time amounted to $90,580,873.00.

science & technology

Transcontinental telegraph service eliminated the Pony Express.

President Lincoln received the first coast-to-coast telegram from Sacramento.

arts & culture

Mrs. Julia Ward Howe wrote the "Battle Hymn of the Republic."

The American Miners' Association was formed in St. Louis.

1862

politics

General Robert E. Lee was appointed Confederate Commander of Armies.

The Department of Agriculture was formed.

The Bureau of Printing and Engraving began.

President Lincoln passed the Homestead Act.

Chief Little Crow led a Sioux uprising in Minnesota.

Congress enacted an anti-polygamy measure aimed at the Mormons in Utah.

Battles were fought at Pea Ridge, Shiloh, Seven Pines and Cedar Mount.

The *Virginia (Merrimac)* sank two Union frigates at Hampton Roads, VA.

Congress established the rank of admiral in the Navy.

Admiral Farragut took possession of New Orleans after a battle with Confederate ships.

The number of men in the Union Army at this time was 575,917.

Andrew Johnson was named military governor of Tennessee.

Martin Van Buren died at the age of 79.

John Tyler died at the age of 72.

The 1862-1867 Sioux Indian War was fought in Minnesota and Dakota.

The first land mines were used in war.

The existence of a rock salt mass was revealed at a mine near New Iberia, LA.

Congress chartered the building of the Union Pacific Railroad.

Public debt rose to $524,176,412.12.

science & technology

A patent was issued to R.J. Gatling for the first machine gun.

John D. Rockefeller, at the age of 23, invested $4,000 of his savings in an oil refining partnership in Cleveland.

A.T. Stewart built a store in New York City which later became Wanamaker's.

Chicago surpassed Cincinnati as the U.S. meat production center.

The nickel industry in the U.S. began when the Lancaster Gap Mine in Pennsylvania began supplying metal for nickel coins.

A.M. Dunham began commercial snowshoe production in Norway, ME.

arts & culture

The Golden Age was the first newspaper in Idaho.

Artist Thomas Nast began what is now political cartooning.

1863

politics

West Virginia was admitted as the thirty-fifth state.

President Lincoln delivered the Gettysburg Address.

President Lincoln issued the Emancipation Proclamation.

The Territory of Arizona was created from the Territory of New Mexico.

The Territory of Idaho was carved from the territories of Washington, Utah, Dakota and Nebraska.

Congress passed the first National Conscription Act.

Anti-draft riots broke out in New York City. Nearly 1,000 were killed or wounded.

Congress established the Office of Comptroller of Currency.

A total of 174,524 immigrants arrived in the U.S.

Income tax receipts in the U.S. amounted to $2,741,857.00.

The Union forces were composed of 918,191 men.

The Confederate invasion of the North ended.

The Union and Confederate campaigns continued.

War broke out with Cheyenne and other Indian tribes in Nebraska, Colorado and the Indian Territory.

Congress authorized the organization of national banks.

The Confederate States tried to break the blockade around southern cities with submarines.

Congress created the National Academy of Science.

General Stonewall Jackson was accidentally shot by his own soldiers.

James A. Garfield was elected to the U.S. House of Representatives.

The national debt rose to $1,119,772,138.00.

science & technology

Ebenezer Butterick invented the first paper dress patterns in the U.S.

The steel age began with a new method of converting iron to steel.

religion

The Mormon Tabernacle was built in Salt Lake City between 1863 and 1867.

arts & culture

Everett Hale's *Man Without a Country* was published.

Henry Wadsworth Longfellow published *Tales of a Wayside Inn, Part I.*

The song "When Johnny Comes Marching Home" was published by L. Lambert.

The *Daily Telegraph* was the first newspaper printed in Wyoming.

1864

politics

Nevada became the thirty-sixth state.

The motto "In God We Trust" was first used on U.S. coins.

Congress amended the National Bank Act replacing the Independent Treasury System of 1846 with a system more attractive to private finance.

General Ulysses S. Grant was named Commander-in-Chief of the Union Armies.

The famous words "Damn the torpedoes! Full speed ahead," were spoken by Admiral Farragut at Mobile Bay.

General Sherman made his famous march to the sea via Atlanta, GA.

A total of 193,195 immigrants arrived in the U.S.

A federal cigarette tax was enacted.

Postal cars began appearing on railroads in Chicago.

General McClellan resigned his commission to run for president.

The Territory of Montana was formed from the Territory of Idaho.

Battles were fought at Olustee, Ft. Pillow, Wilderness, Chickamauga, Cold Harbor, Spottsylvania, Petersburg, and Cedar Creek.

Arkansas adopted the motto "Regnant Populi" (The People Rule).

Montana adopted the motto "Oro y Plata" (Gold and Silver).

Rhode Island adopted the motto "Hope."

The Confederate cruiser *Alabama* was sunk near France by the U.S.S *Kearsarge*.

The national debt at this time amounted to $1,815,784,370.00.

science & technology

The casualty insurance industry began in Hartford, CT.

G.P. Rowell began the first successful advertising agency in the U.S.

arts & culture

The songs "Beautiful Dreamer" and "Tramp, Tramp, Tramp" were published.

Songster Stephen Foster died at the age of 38.

Novelist Nathaniel Hawthorne died at the age of 60.

The Red Cross was founded in Geneva, Switzerland.

The *Montana Post* was the first newspaper in the Montana Territory.

the *Frontier Scout* was the first newspaper published in North Dakota.

1865

politics

President Lincoln was inaugurated for his second term. Andrew Johnson was his vice president.

The Civil War ended when General Robert E. Lee surrendered to General Ulysses S. Grant at the Appomattox Court House, VA on April 9.

President Lincoln was assassinated by John Wilkes Booth on April 14th. He was the first president to be assassinated.

Andrew Johnson became the seventeenth president upon the death of President Lincoln.

The total death toll of the war was 524,509—359,528 Union soldiers and 164,981 Confederate.

The number of dollars in circulation in the U.S. at this time was 1,081,540,514.

A total of 247,453 immigrants arrived in the U.S.

Income tax receipts amounted to $32,050,917.00.

A total of $8,525,153.00 was paid out in government pensions.

The Thirteenth Amendment to the Constitution, abolishing slavery, was adopted.

The president rescinded the restriction of trade west of the Mississippi River.

Confederate President Jefferson Davis was imprisoned at Ft. Monroe, VA.

There were about 295,000 Indians in the U.S. at this time. In 1492, there had been approximately 850,000.

The national debt at this time was $2,680,869,000.00.

science & technology

A company in Fredonia, NY was the first to sell natural gas in the U.S.

The first American cannery was built on the Pacific Coast.

The Butterfield Overland Dispatch was formed to take passengers and packages between the Missouri River and Denver.

The Southern Pacific Railroad was chartered.

The compression ice machine was invented by Thaddeus Lowe.

arts & culture

"The Celebrated Jumping Frog of Calaveras County" made Mark Twain famous.

Walt Whitman wrote "Drum Taps."

The Ku Klux Klan was first formed in Pulaski, TN.

Mascara came into vogue.

The *San Francisco Examiner* was first published by William Moss.

1866

politics

Congress authorized the issuance of a 5¢ coin known as the nickel.

The first formal observance of Lincoln's birthday was held in Washington, DC.

The first national encampment of the Union of Veterans of the Civil War was held in Indianapolis, IN.

Lieutenant Colonel Custer was sent to quell uprisings led by Sioux Indian Chiefs Sitting Bull and Crazy Horse.

The first Civil Rights Act was passed to safeguard civil rights within states.

A total of 163,594 immigrants arrived in the U.S.

Income tax receipts totaled $72,982,160.00.

A total of $15,450,549.00 was paid out in government pensions.

Nevada adopted the motto "All for Our Country."

Idaho adopted the motto "Salve" (Welcome).

Vermont adopted the motto "Freedom and Unity."

Boise, ID was established.

President Johnson came into open opposition to Congress.

The national debt at this time was $2,773,236,173.00.

Some 250,000 cattle were driven from Texas to Sedalia, MO on the Sedalia Trail.

science & technology

The final laying of an Atlantic cable between the U.S. and Great Britain was completed.

The first elevated railroad in the U.S. was built in New York City.

The first tin can with a key opener was patented.

The first dynamite was manufactured in San Francisco.

religion

Christian Science was founded by Mary Baker Eddy.

arts & culture

The song "When You and I Were Young, Maggie" was published.

M.I.T. began the first architecture course in a U.S. college.

The first American Society for the Prevention of Cruelty to Animals was formed in New York.

A fire in Portland, ME caused $10 million in damage.

Newport, RI opened the first skating rink in America.

1867

politics

Nebraska became the thirty-seventh state.

Nebraska adopted the motto "Equality Before the Law."

President Johnson extended amnesty to all but a few Confederate leaders.

The U.S. agreed to purchase Alaska from Russia for $7.5 million (about 2¢ an acre). The purchase became known as "Seward's Folly."

Minneapolis, MN was established.

Cheyenne, WY was established with the advance of the Union Pacific Railroad.

Passage of the Reconstruction Acts began. These acts of Congress, passed from 1867 to 1877, provided for the reorganization of the former Confederate States and set forth the process by which they were to be restored representation in Congress.

The U.S. experienced an economic depression.

Enlistment in the Army during peacetime was set at 54,641.

Northerners who exploited the favorable economic and political conditions in the South after the Civil War became known as carpetbaggers.

U.S. troops began a campaign against the Comanche, Lipan, Kiowa and Kickapoo Indians which would last until 1881.

Midway Island was occupied by the U.S.

Tucson was made the capital of the Arizona Territory.

Rutherford B. Hayes was elected Governor of Ohio.

A total of 298,967 immigrants arrived in the U.S.

The national debt at this time was $2,678,126,103.00.

science & technology

The Pullman's Palace Car Co. was incorporated.

The first refrigerated car was patented by J.B. Sutherland of Detroit.

Ticker tape machines were installed at the New York Stock Exchange.

arts & culture

The cattle route from San Antonio, TX to Abilene, KS became known as the Chisholm Trail.

Charles Weller, a court reporter, created the slogan "Now is the time for all good men to come to the aid of their party" to test typewriters.

The Benevolent and Protective Order of Elks (B.P.O.E.) was founded.

1868

politics

President Johnson was acquitted in impeachment proceedings which were initiated by Congessmen who objected to Johnson's policy of military reconstruction and black suffrage.

The Fourteenth Amendment was adopted, granting citizenship to blacks.

The treason trial of Jefferson Davis began. It was dropped in 1869.

Former president James Buchanan died at the age of 77 in Lancaster, PA.

May 30, Decoration Day, was celebrated nationally for the first time.

Major J.W. Powell began a survey of the Grand Canyon and the Colorado River.

A great wave of homesteaders began settling the Nebraska region.

A total of $23,101,509.00 was paid out in government pensions.

Income tax receipts for the year amounted to $41,455,599.00.

A total of 282,189 immigrants arrived in the U.S.

science & technology

The open-hearth process in the American steel industry began in Trenton, NJ.

George Westinghouse's air brake was first used on passenger trains.

J.B. Eads first used steel in bridge building.

A.M. Hills invented the lawn mower.

The first tape measure was patented.

The first elevator was installed in an office building in New York City.

arts & culture

Little Women by Louisa May Alcott became a best-seller in Boston.

The song "The Flying Trapeze" was popular at this time.

Letter carriers' uniforms were approved.

The first indoor amateur track and field meet was held in New York City.

The *Atlanta Constitution* was founded as a daily newspaper.

Cornell University in Ithaca, NY established the first veterinary school in the U.S.

Baseball uniforms were introduced by the Cincinnati Red Stockings.

1869

politics

Ulysses S. Grant was inaugurated as the eighteenth president. Schuyler Colfax was his vice president.

William F. Cody became known as "Buffalo Bill."

The first women's suffrage (voting rights) in the U.S. was granted in the Wyoming Territory.

The first caricature of Uncle Sam with chin whiskers appeared in *Harper's Weekly*.

Franklin Pierce died at the age of 64.

The first state board of health in the U.S. was founded in Massachusetts.

The "Black Friday" financial panic occurred in New York City on September 24th when stock gamblers Jay Gould and James Fisk tried to corner the U.S. gold supply.

The U.S. Army at this time had 14,000 Indian fighters deployed from Texas to North Dakota.

Massachusetts established the first state bureau of labor in the U.S.

A total of 352,569 immigrants arrived in the U.S.

Income tax receipts for the year totaled $34,791,857.00.

A total of $28,513,247.00 was paid out in government pensions.

The U.S. leased the Pribilof Islands.

The national debt at this time was $2,588,452,213.00.

science & technology

H.J. Heinz and L.C. Noble established a food packing company in Pennsylvania. Their first product was grated horseradish.

The first patent for chewing gum was issued.

The first transcontinental railroad was completed at Promontory Point, UT.

The first patent for a suction principle vacuum cleaner was issued.

arts & culture

The songs "Now the Day Is Over" and "Little Brown Jug" were published.

Mark Twain's *The Innocents Abroad* was published.

The *Sitka Times* was the first newspaper published in Alaska.

The first baseball team to pay its players salaries was the Cincinnati Red Stockings.

From 1854 to 1869, Wells Fargo Express Co. suffered 313 stagecoach robberies.

The Brooklyn Bridge was begun in New York.

Bicycling was enjoying popularity at this time.

Arabella Mansfield, the first woman lawyer in the U.S. since colonial times, was admitted to the Iowa Bar.

The hoopskirt gave way to the bustle at about this time.

1870

The population of the 37 states at this time was 39,818,449.

The donkey as the symbol of the Democratic Party was first published in a *Harper's Weekly* cartoon.

Women voted for the first time in America in a Utah election.

The Fifteenth Amendment was adopted, which stated that no citizen should be deprived of the right to vote because of race.

Congress created the U.S. Weather Bureau and the Justice Department.

U.S. Senator H.R. Revels from Mississippi was the first black in Congress.

A total of 387,292 immigrants arrived in the U.S.

The estimated wealth of the nation at this time was $30,068,518,000.00.

Grover Cleveland was the sheriff of Erie County, NY at this time.

William McKinley was a prosecuting attorney in Ohio.

General Robert E. Lee died at the age of 69 in Portsmouth, NH.

Income tax receipts for the year totaled $37,775,872.00.

The total amount paid out in government pensions for the year was $29,351,488.00

Georgia was the first state to return to the Union after the Civil War.

By now there were 49,168 miles of railroad track in the U.S.

The National Education Association was formed.

The national debt at this time was $2,480,672,427.00

Cellophane was patented.

Labor Union membership in the U.S. at this time was 300,000.

John D. and William Rockefeller were the principal organizers of the Standard Oil Co.

The first brick paving was laid in Charleston, WV.

Sand blasting was patented.

The Pullman Company completed its first transcontinental journey.

The Great Atlantic & Pacific Tea Co. was formed.

The Denver & Rio Grande Railway was incorporated.

1871

politics

Calvin Coolidge was born in Plymouth, VT.

William Jennings Bryan delivered his first recorded political speech in Centralia, IL, at the age of 12.

A total of 404,806 immigrants arrived in the U.S.

Income tax receipts for the year amounted to $14,436,861.00.

A total of $29,752,746.00 was paid out in government pensions.

Dodge City, KS sprang up with the completion of the Atchison, Topeka & Santa Fe Railway.

The Boot Hill cemetery in Dodge City became well-known as the burial place for many famous outlaws and gunfighters.

The Modoc War was the last Indian war to effect southern Oregon and northern California.

Congress founded the *Congressional Record*, a journal of its daily proceedings.

The first Arbor Day was celebrated in Nebraska.

California authorized the first bird refuge in Oakland.

The Union was completely restored after the Civil War.

President Ulysses S. Grant became known as "Unconditional Surrender" Grant because of his role in the Civil War.

King Kamehameha V, who decreed the new constitution for Hawaii, died.

The national debt at this time was $2,253,251,328.00.

science & technology

The first doughnut cutter was patented in Thomaston, ME.

The first air brake was patented by George Westinghouse, Jr.

The first mercantile corporation in the U.S. was formed at St. Louis, MO.

Montgomery Ward & Co., the first mail order house in the U.S., opened in Chicago.

The first cigarette manufacturing machine was invented.

Robinson invented block signals for railroads.

Dried milk was patented.

religion

The Russian Orthodox Church transferred its Episcopal See from Alaska to San Francisco.

Mormons trekked through the Painted Desert in Arizona and settled on the Little Colorado River.

The Jehovah's Witnesses were organized by Charles T. Russell.

1872

politics

President Grant established the first civil service commission.

The U.S. Bureau of Fisheries was established.

Lincoln, NE was established.

A total of 321,350 immigrants arrived in the U.S.

The expenses of the 1870 census amounted to $3,287,000.00.

At this time there were 53,000 federal employees. By 1900 there would be 256,000.

Between 1850 and 1870, the U.S. Government gave 200 million acres of public land to the railroads.

Congress passed the Indian Appropriation Act, which made all Indians national wards and nullified all Indian treaties.

The Lifesaving Service was introduced.

The national debt at this time was $2,353,211,332.00.

science & technology

The word "blizzard" was first used to describe snowstorms with strong winds.

Cement was patented.

The St. Louis-Southwest Railroad was chartered.

The first municipal gas plant was acquired by Wheeling, WV.

The first corrugated paper was patented.

The Northern Pacific Railway reached Fargo, ND.

The first seedless naval oranges were imported from Brazil.

The carousel was patented.

religion

Mormon leader Brigham Young was arrested for polygamy (the practice of being married to more than one person).

The hymn "Onward Christian Soldiers" was published.

arts & culture

The famous Chicago fire, started by Mrs. O'Leary's cow, caused $200 million worth of damage.

The first Grand Central Station opened in New York City. It was replaced in 1913.

The first professional baseball association was organized, replacing the National Amateur Association.

P.T. Barnum organized his circus, "The Greatest Show on Earth."

The first boardwalk in the world was completed in Atlantic City, NJ.

1873

politics

President Grant was inaugurated for his second term. Henry Wilson was his vice president.

The first Americans scaled Mt. Whitney, the highest mountain in the contiguous U.S.

A total of 459,803 immigrants arrived in the U.S.

Income tax receipts for the year totaled $5,062,312.00

A total of $26,982,063.00 was paid out in government pensions.

The American Military Commission recommended the building of a naval station at Pearl Harbor, HI.

El Paso, TX was established.

The building of railroads put an end to the long Texas cattle drives.

The discovery of silver in Nevada started another mining rush.

The U.S. Government issued 1¢ post cards.

The national debt at this time was $2,234,482,993.00.

science & technology

A.S. Hallidie invented the cable car. It was first used in San Francisco.

The Pullman Company introduced gas lights on trains.

J.W. Carhart built the first automobile in the U.S. in Racine, WI.

The first linoleum was manufactured in Richmond, NY.

The slicing machine was patented.

J.F. Glidden of Illinois patented the first successful barbed wire.

religion

The Union of American Hebrew Congregations was organized.

arts & culture

Jules Verne published *Around the World in Eighty Days.*

"Bookmakers" (professionals who place bets for gamblers) first appeared at U.S. race tracks.

"Survivor" won the first annual Preakness Stakes at Pimlico, MD.

Bellevue Hospital in New York established its school of nursing, following the principles of Florence Nightingale.

The Women's Christian Temperance Union was organized.

The first football rules were formulated in New York City.

1874

politics

The elephant was used for the first time as the symbol of the Republican Party in *Harper's Weekly*.

Herbert Hoover was born in West Branch, IA.

The territorial government of the District of Columbia was abolished and replaced by a commission.

A total of 313,339 immigrants arrived in the U.S.

Income tax receipts for the year totaled $140,391.00.

A total of $30,206,778.00 was paid out in government pensions.

U.S. Army headquarters was moved to St. Louis, MO.

The Red River Indian War was fought in the Indian Territory with the Kiowa, Cheyenne and Commanche Indiand.

The national debt at this time was $2,251,690,468.00.

science & technology

The medical discipline of osteopathy was developed by Dr. A.D. Still of Baldwin, KS.

The first corset was manufactured as a health item.

The first electric streetcar made a successful run in New York City.

R.J. Reynolds built his first factory in Winston-Salem, NC.

Washington Duke & Sons built their first factory at Durham, NC.

The first steel arch bridge was opened in St. Louis, MO.

The first adhesive and medical plaster were successfully manufactured in East Orange, NJ.

The first tin factory was established in Leechburg, PA.

Sargent & Greenleaf manufactured the first time lock.

Mennonites from Russia introduced Turkey Red wheat to Kansas.

religion

The hymn "I Love to Tell the Story" was published.

arts & culture

The Philadelphia Zoological Gardens opened. It was the first public zoo in the U.S.

The ice cream soda was introduced by R.M. Green of Philadelphia.

The first football goal posts were used at Cambridge, MA.

1875

politics

Congress passed the Civil Rights Act, giving blacks equal rights in public places.

The American Forestry Association was founded in Chicago.

A total of 227,498 immigrants arrived in the U.S.

The International Bureau of Weights and Measures was established in Paris, France.

Dodge City, KS prospered as a notorious frontier town and cattle shipping point on the Santa Fe Trail.

The Sons of the American Revolution was formed.

The twenty-one gun salute was adopted by the U.S. from British custom.

Andrew Johnson died at the age of 66 and was buried in Greenville, TN.

The national debt at this time was $2,232,284,531.00.

science & technology

The railroad was completed from Brooklyn to Coney Island, NY, leading to its becoming a famous seaside resort.

The rotary printing press, which printed on both sides of a sheet at the same time, was invented by S.D. Tucker and A. Campbell.

The first shipments of dressed beef from the Great Plains to Europe began.

The dynamo was invented by Charles G. Brush of Cleveland, OH.

The National Bankers' Association was organized.

The first oat-crushing machine was patented.

The first electric drill was patented by G.F. Green.

The first folding bed was manufactured.

religion

Mary Baker Eddy published *Science and Health with a Key to the Scriptures*.

The Theosophical Society was founded in New York by Helena Blavatsky.

The first American cardinal, Archbishop John McCloskey, was invested in St. Patrick's Cathedral in New York City.

arts & culture

The baseball glove was introduced by C.G. Waite, a first baseman for a Boston team.

The first newspaper cartoon strip appeared in the *Daily Graphic*.

The first football uniforms were worn at a game between Harvard and Tufts Universities.

The first Kentucky Derby was held at Churchill Downs, KY.

1876

politics

Colorado was admitted as the thirty-eighth state. It was known as the Centennial State.

General George A. Custer and all 256 men of the 7th Cavalry were slaughtered by Sioux Indians led by Sitting Bull at Little Big Horn in the Montana Territory.

The American Library Association was founded in Philadelphia.

A Centennial Exposition was held in Philadelphia.

Gold was discovered south of Juneau, AK.

The 1876-1879 Sioux and Cheyenne War was fought.

A total of 169,986 immigrants arrived in the U.S.

The Homestake Mine, the "world's greatest gold mine," was discovered at Lead, SD.

The national debt at this time was $2,180,395,067.00.

science & technology

The first photograph of the solar spectrum was taken by an astronomer in New York City.

Thomas Edison invented the mimeograph.

The first U.S. patent for the telephone was awarded to Alexander Graham Bell.

religion

The hymn "What a Friend We Have in Jesus" was published.

arts & culture

Mark Twain's *The Adventures of Tom Sawyer* was published.

Henry James published *Roderick Hudson*.

The song "I'll Take You Home Again, Kathleen" was published.

Oscar Hammerstein entered the theater business in New York City.

Wild Bill Hickok was shot and killed in Deadwood, SD.

The first U.S. cooking school was opened in New York.

Polo was first played in America in New York City.

The first fraternity house in the U.S. opened at Williams College in Massachusetts.

The National League of Baseball was formed.

The Imperial Council of the Ancient Arabic Order of Nobles of the Mystic Shrine was organized in the U.S.

1877

politics

Rutherford B. Hayes was inaugurated as the nineteenth president. William A. Wheeler was his vice president.

H.O. Flipper was the first black man to graduate from West Point Military Academy.

Flag Day was observed for the first time marking the 100th anniversary of the U.S. flag.

A total of 141,857 immigrants arrived in the U.S.

President Hayes recalled federal troops from the southern states.

Political reconstruction ended in the South with the withdrawal of federal troops.

The government intensified its campaign against "moonshine" whiskey.

Forts Missoula, Keogh and Custer were constructed in the Montana Territory.

Congress passed the Desert Land Act, making large plots of land available at a very low price in order to encourage settlement and reclamation of desert areas in the U.S.

William McKinley was elected to the U.S. House of Representatives.

The first prison for women opened in Sherborn, MA.

A total of $28,182,821.00 was paid out in government pensions.

The term "first lady of the land" was first applied to President Hayes' wife, Lucy.

The national debt at this time was $2,205,301,392.00.

science & technology

Thomas Edison patented the phonograph.

The first telephone exchange was established in Boston.

Asphalt paving was first laid in New York.

The first bicycle factory was established in Hartford, CT.

There were now 3,000 telephones in operation in the U.S.

The first centrifugal cream separator was patented.

J.T. Appleby patented the knotter, which tied bundles of grain with twine.

The American Chemical Society was chartered.

religion

Mormon Church leader Brigham Young died at the age of 76.

arts & culture

Charles E. Hires began making and distributing root beer.

The American Humane was formed in Cleveland, OH.

Henry James published *The American*.

1878

politics

The Bland-Allison Act was passed reestablishing bimetallism (currency based on gold and silver values) in an effort by Congress to remedy the depressed economy.

A total of 138,469 immigrants arrived in the U.S.

The first Portuguese contract laborers arrived in Hawaii.

The Washington Territory, striving for statehood, framed its first constitution.

Kansas experienced its last Indian raid in Decatur County.

The national debt at this time amounted to $2,210,553,530.00.

science & technology

The first electrical light company was the Edison Electric Light Co. in New York City.

The first regular telephone exchange opened in New Haven, CT.

The first dirigible (airship) made in the U.S. flew in Lancaster, PA.

Thomas Edison announced the incandescent lamp.

The corncob pipe, patented by H. Tribbe, was first commercially manufactured.

Mechanical cold storage of fruits was first applied.

arts & culture

The French opera *Carmen* made its U.S. debut in New York City.

Anna K. Green's novel *The Leavenworth Case* set the formula for modern detective stories.

The song "Carry Me Back to Old Virginny" was published.

The American Bar Association was formed at Saratoga, NY.

Over 5,000 people in Memphis and 4,000 in New Orleans died of yellow fever.

The National Archery Association was formed.

The first successful Sunday edition of a daily newspaper was published in Philadelphia.

Milk in glass bottles was first delivered in Brooklyn, NY.

The first auto race was won by A. Gallagher, who drove from Green Bay to Madison, WI at an average speed of six miles per hour.

The first bicycle club was formed in Boston.

E.N. Nutt of Boston became the first woman telephone operator.

The first telephone directory was issued in New Haven, CT.

1879

politics

The Ute Indians of Colorado staged an armed uprising and moved to Utah.

The U.S. Geographical Survey was created as part of the Department of the Interior.

A total of 177,826 immigrants arrived in the U.S.

B.A. Lockwood was the first woman admitted to practice law before the U.S. Supreme Court.

There was an extensive exodus to Kansas from the southern states by blacks.

Squatters from Missouri and Texas in the Oklahoma Territory were ordered to move by the president.

Lieutenant G.W. DeLong and his men all perished in their attempt to reach the North Pole by way of the Bering Strait.

The U.S. concluded an alliance with Spain.

The government issued the first postage-due stamps.

The national debt at this time was $2,249,567,482.00.

science & technology

The first cash register was patented by J.J. Ritty of Dayton, OH.

F.W. Woolworth opened the first successful 5 & 10¢ store in Utica, NY.

The Archaeological Institute of America was organized in Boston.

Thomas Edison filed for a patent for his incandescent lamp.

Saccharin (an artificial sweetener) was discovered in Baltimore, MD.

The first hanging railroad bridge was built at Canon City, CO.

G.B. Selden filed for the first patent on the automobile. He did not receive a patent until 1895.

religion

Mary Baker Eddy established the First Church of Christ Scientist in Boston.

arts & culture

Henry James published his novella *Daisy Miller.*

Gilbert and Sullivan's *H.M.S. Pinafore* opened in New York City.

The first indoor ice skating rink opened in New York City.

The University of Missouri at Columbia organized the first journalism course.

Richmond and Cleveland played the first no-hitter baseball game on record.

1880

politics

The population of the 38 states was 50,155,783.

The first major gold strike in Alaska led to the development of Juneau.

A total of 457,257 immigrants arrived in the U.S.

The estimated national wealth at this time was $43,642,000,000.00.

A total of $56,689,299.00 was paid out in government pensions.

By now, many associations of ranchers from Texas to Canada were consolidating water rights, thus creating princely domains among ranchers.

The national debt at this time was $2,120,415,370.00.

science & technology

The American Society of Mechanical Engineers was formed.

The first successful roll film for cameras was patented by George Eastman.

The safety razor was developed by the Kempfe brothers.

The Sherwin-Williams Company began manufacturing house paint.

Thomas Edison was granted a patent for his incandescent lamp.

The Bell telephone system was introduced in Hawaii.

Over 8,000 cases of salmon were packed and shipped in Alaska.

The clay pigeon target was patented for trapshooting.

The first pay station telephone service was established in New Haven, CT.

religion

The American branch of the Salvation Army was founded in Pennsylvania.

arts & culture

The first portion of the Metropolitan Museum of Art opened in New York City.

John Philip Sousa was made leader of the U.S. Marine Band.

Lillian Russell made her stage debut in New York.

The National Croquet League was formed.

The first canoe association was formed at Lake George, NY.

The phrase "Let the chips fall where they may" came into use at about this time.

1881

politics

James A. Garfield was inaugurated as the twentieth president. Chester A. Arthur was his vice president.

President Garfield died of gunshot wounds in a Washington, DC railroad station.

Chester A. Arthur became the twenty-first president upon Garfield's death.

The Texas state capital building burned.

Clara Barton organized the American National Red Cross in Washington, DC.

A total of 669,431 immigrants arrived in the U.S.

A celebration of the 100th anniversary of Cornwallis' surrender was held in Yorktown, VA.

Spokane, WA and Helena, MT were established.

Chief Sitting Bull surrendered in North Dakota.

By now, over 100 million pounds of beef were being sent from the Great Plains to Europe annually.

The first Norwegian contract laborers arrived in Hawaii.

Grover Cleveland was elected mayor of Buffalo, NY.

The American Federation of Labor was organized.

The California legislature enacted a quarantine on plants in order to protect local crops from infestation.

The national debt at this time was $2,120,415,370.00.

science & technology

Thomas Edison directed construction of the first central electric light plant in the world at New York City.

The catch of whales in Alaskan waters was valued at $1,139,000.00.

religion

The Christian Endeavor, an organization for young people, was formed in Portland, ME.

arts & culture

Henry James published *Portrait of a Lady*.

The first player piano was patented.

American Angler became the first American fishing journal.

The U.S. Lawn Tennis Association was formed.

Coney Island in New York began to be known as a resort at about this time.

The Barnum & Bailey Circus was formed by a merger.

The Knights of the Macabees was introduced in the U.S.

1882

politics

Franklin D. Roosevelt was born in Hyde Park, NY.

The first Chinese Exclusion Act barred Chinese labor for ten years.

A total of $54,313,172.00 was paid out in government pensions.

The U.S. Government was defrauded out of $4 million in the Star Route Frauds.

The Iolani Palace in Hawaii was completed.

Theodore Roosevelt was elected to the New York legislature.

A total of 788,992 immigrants arrived in the U.S.

A bicentennial celebration was held in Philadelphia to commemorate William Penn's landing there.

Labor Day was first observed in New York. It later became a national holiday.

The national debt at this time was $1,918,312,994.00.

science & technology

H.W. Seely patented the electric flat iron.

S.S. Wheeler patented the electric fan.

The first hydroelectric plant in the U.S. was built in Appleton, WI.

The Great Northern Railroad was completed through the Red River Valley to Canada.

Commercial herring fishing began in southeast Alaska.

The East River Bridge opened between New York and Brooklyn.

religion

The Knights of Columbus was organized at New Haven, CT.

arts & culture

Mark Twain published *The Prince and the Pauper*.

Poets Henry Wadsworth Longfellow and Ralph Waldo Emerson died.

Western bank robber and murderer Jesse James was killed.

Malted milk was introduced by William Horlick of Racine, WI.

The first handball court in America was built by Phil Casey.

John L. Sullivan won the American heavyweight boxing championship from Paddy Ryan. At this time boxing was done with bare fists.

The first major league baseball game was played between Providence and Worcester.

1883

politics	*science & technology*	*arts & culture*

Tacoma, WA was established.

Santa Fe, NM celebrated its 333rd anniversary.

A total of 603,322 immigrants arrived in the U.S.

Teddy Roosevelt moved to North Dakota for his health and began ranching near Medora.

Liberty head nickels came into circulation.

Grover Cleveland was elected governor of New York.

The Civil Service Commission was established by the Pendleton Act.

Congress acted to reduce postage to 2¢ per half-ounce.

The national debt at this time was $1,884,171,728.07.

A patent was issued for the first practical cigar rolling machine.

The first telephone service between New York and Chicago was initiated.

The linotype was invented by Ottman Mergenthaler.

The Northern Pacific Railroad was completed at Goldcreek, MT.

The highest masonry building in the U.S. was erected in Chicago. It was 16 stories high.

The electric elevated railroad was begun in Chicago.

The wire woven fence was introduced by J.W. Page in Lenawee County, MI.

Vaudeville was introduced in the U.S. by Benjamin Franklin Keith in Boston.

The *Ladies' Home Journal* was established.

The Metropolitan Opera House in New York City opened.

The song "There's a Tavern on the Green" was popular at this time.

Buffalo Bill Cody began performing with the first Wild West Show at North Platte, NE.

The first baseball game played under electric lights was at Fort Wayne, IN.

The modern Woodmen of America was founded in Lyons, IA.

★ ★ ★ ★

1884

politics

The cornerstone for the pedestal of the Statue of Liberty was laid at Bedloe's Island, NY.

Harry S. Truman was born near Lamar, MO.

A total of $57,912,387.00 was paid out in government pensions.

The U.S. Bureau of Labor was created as a part of the Department of the Interior.

A civil government was established in Alaska.

A total of 518,592 immigrants arrived in the U.S.

The International Prime Meridian Conference in Washington, DC set Greenwich as the prime meridian.

The first American governor of Alaska was appointed.

The capstone of the Washington Monument was placed in Washington, DC.

By this time it was estimated that over $30 million of British capital had been invested in ranching on the Great Plains.

In response to being drafted as a presidential candidate, William T. Sherman wrote, "I will not accept if nominated, and will not serve if elected."

The slogan "Rum, Romanism, and Rebellion" (stated by Republican candidate James G. Blaine in reference to the heavily Irish-American Democratic Party) helped Grover Cleveland win the presidential election.

The name "mugwumps" was given to Republicans who betrayed the party to support Cleveland.

The national debt at this time was $1,830,528,923.00.

science & technology

The first steel-skeleton construction began in Chicago. This type of construction permitted the building of skyscrapers.

William W. Keen performed the first successful operation to remove a brain tumor in the U.S.

The American Institute of Electrical Engineers was founded.

The first practical fountain pen was invented by L.E. Waterman.

The first glider flight was made in Otay, CA by J.J. Montgomery.

arts & culture

Mark Twain wrote *The Adventures of Huckleberry Finn*.

Greyhound racing was introduced at Philadelphia.

S.S. McClure founded the first newspaper syndicate in the U.S.

The first U.S. state college for women was founded at Columbus, MS.

The Ringling Bros. Circus began performing.

1885

politics

Grover Cleveland was inaugurated as the twenty-second president. Thomas A. Hendricks was his vice president.

The U.S. Post Office established a special delivery service.

The Statue of Liberty was shipped in sections from France.

The Washington Monument was dedicated, 37 years after the laying of the cornerstone.

Ulysses S. Grant died at the age of 63 and was buried in New York City.

A total of 395,346 immigrants arrived in the U.S.

There was an outbreak of attacks by Apache Indians under Chief Geronimo in Arizona and New Mexico.

Miners at Rock Springs, WY massacred Chinese miners.

At this time, 550,000 people lived in the Dakota Territory.

The U.S. experienced an economic depression.

In the 1880s, there was a great deal of conflict between the U.S., Canada and Japan over seal fishing in the Bering Sea.

There were now 128,967 miles of railroad track in the U.S.

Charleston became the capital of West Virginia.

science & technology

The first "piggyback" railroad operation was done by the Long Island Railroad Company.

U.S. coal production now exceeded 100 million tons a year.

The first paper mill in the Pacific Northwest was established at Camas in the Washington Territory.

The American Telephone & Telegraph Company (AT&T) was organized.

The first appendectomy operation was performed in Davenport, IA.

First aid instruction was first offered in Peekskill, NY.

The first commercially operated streetcars ran in Baltimore, MD.

arts & culture

Scott Joplin, composer of ragtime music, began playing piano in St. Louis.

Norwegian settlers in Wisconsin and Minnesota brought the sport of skiing to America.

1886

politics

The Statue of Liberty was unveiled and dedicated by President Cleveland.

Brothers Robert L. and Alfred A. Taylor competed for the governorship of Tennessee.

The U.S. experienced labor troubles throughout the country.

President Grover Cleveland and Miss Francis Folsom were married in the White House.

Chester A. Arthur died at the age of 56 and was buried at Albany, NY.

A total of 334,203 immigrants arrived in the U.S.

Chinese settlers were driven out of Seattle in the Washington Territory. U.S. troops were called in to restore order.

Kansas City, KS was established.

Apache Indian Chief Geronimo was captured in Arizona, which virtually ended Navajo and Apache Indian fighting in the U.S. and Mexico.

The United Mine Workers were organized.

Alcatraz Island in San Francisco Bay became a military prison.

Congress approved the incorporation of the National Trade Unions.

The national debt at this time amounted to $1,775,063,013.00.

science & technology

The Big Bend Tunnel, which was two miles long, was opened in California.

Smokeless gunpowder was invented.

Westinghouse Electric and Manufacturing Co. was organized.

The electric welding machine was patented.

A linotype was successfully operated by the *New York Tribune*.

The first typewriter ribbon was patented in Memphis, TN.

arts & culture

The Bostonians by Henry James was published.

Cosmopolitan magazine was founded in New York.

Little Lord Fauntleroy was published.

The first issue of *The World Almanac and Book of Facts* went on sale.

The Valley Hunt Club staged the first Tournament of Roses in Pasadena, CA.

An earthquake in Charleston, SC destroyed $5 million worth of property.

1887

politics

Free delivery of mail was provided to all communities of 10,000 or more.

Pearl Harbor was leased from Hawaii as a naval station.

The Interstate Commerce Commission was established.

The state of New York legalized betting at the racetrack.

Labor Day was first observed as a legal holiday in New York.

A total of 490,109 immigrants arrived in the U.S.

Jacksonville, FL was established.

Congress organized the Hospital Corps in the U.S. Army.

A total of $73,752,977.00 was paid out in government pensions.

Philadelphia celebrated the creation of the Constitution.

Congress established experimental agricultural stations in several states.

Mrs. Medora Salter of Argonia, KS became the first woman mayor in the U.S.

William H. Taft was a judge in the Ohio Superior Court.

The Dawes Act bestowed U.S. citizenship on American Indians.

The national debt at this time was $1,657,602,592.00.

science & technology

Flat phonograph records were invented by Emile Berliner.

The Columbia Phonograph Co. was founded at Bridgeport, CT.

The first daily railroad service from the Atlantic to the Pacific was established.

Celluloid photographic film was invented by H.W. Goodwin.

The first cancer hospital was opened in New York City.

arts & culture

"Little Boy Blue" was published by Eugene Field.

The American Trotting Association was formed in Detroit, MI.

Blizzards in the winter of 1886-1887 killed 80% to 90% of the cattle on the northern plains.

1888

politics

The secret ballot was first used in America in local elections in Louisville, KY.

Electrocution replaced death by hanging as capital punishment in New York.

Congress established the Department of Labor.

By this time, Oklahoma was heavily populated by Indians.

The population of the Montana Territory was about 140,000; that of the Washington Territory, 350,000; that of the Wyoming Territory, about 60,000.

Congress debated extensively on the formation of trusts in the U.S.

Congress authorized a commission for federal labor arbitration.

The present Texas state capitol building was dedicated.

Belva Ann Lockwood was the first woman to run for president. She ran with the Equal Rights Party.

science & technology

P.W. Pratt designed the first electric automobile in Boston.

The first incubator for infants was built in New York City.

The revolving door was patented in Philadelphia.

A method of measuring the butterfat content in milk was invented by S.M. Babcock.

The ball-point pen was patented by J.J. Loud.

George Eastman perfected the box camera and roll film.

arts & culture

DeWolf Hooper gave the first public recital of "Casey at the Bat" in New York City.

The first saxophone was manufactured in Elkhart, IN.

Violinist Fritz Kreisler made his American debut at the age of 13.

More than 400 people died of yellow fever in Jacksonville, FL.

A 36-hour blizzard struck New York City, killing 400 people and halting transportation and commerce.

The Loyal Order of the Moose was founded in Louisville, KY.

The first competitive rodeo was held in Prescott, AZ.

1889

politics

Benjamin Harrison was inaugurated as the twenty-third president. Levi P. Morton was his vice president.

North Dakota, South Dakota, Montana and Washington were all admitted as states.

The famous Oklahoma land rush by 50,000 people occurred.

The United Confederate Veterans was organized in New Orleans, LA.

Jefferson Davis, ex-president of the Confederate States, died in New Orleans.

Free mail delivery to the home was introduced in cities of 5,000 or more.

Congress established the Department of Agriculture.

Oklahoma City, OK was established.

Georgia was the first state to make Robert E. Lee's birthday a legal holiday.

New York celebrated the centennial of George Washington's inauguration as president.

The national debt at this time was $1,619,052,922.00.

science & technology

The Singer Manufacturing Co. produced the first electric sewing machine known in the U.S.

The first coin telephone was patented by William Gray.

W.J. and C. H. Mayo founded the Mayo Clinic in Rochester, MN.

The first movie film in America was developed by Thomas Edison on a base developed by George Eastman.

The Johns Hopkins Hospital opened in Baltimore, MD.

The first bessemer steel I-beams in the U.S. were produced in Pittsburgh, PA.

arts & culture

Mark Twain published *A Connecticut Yankee in King Arthur's Court.*

John Philip Sousa composed the "Washington Post March."

The first clarinet made of metal was patented.

The Johnstown Flood occurred in Pennsylvania, killing 2,295 when the dam broke.

The first All-American football team was selected by Walter Camp.

The largest dry dock in the world opened at Newport News, VA.

1890

politics

The population of the U.S. at this time was 62,947,714.

Idaho became the forty-third state and Wyoming became the forty-fourth.

Dwight D. Eisenhower was born in Denison, TX.

Congress passed the Sherman Anti-Trust Act prohibiting contracts and agreements that restrained foreign or interstate trade.

From 1820 to 1890, there were 15,641,680 immigrants to the U.S.: 4,551,719 from Germany; 3,501,683 from Ireland; and 2,460,034 from England.

The Federal Government established Yosemite and Sequoia National Parks.

William Jennings Bryan was elected to his first public office in Nebraska.

The Daughters of the American Revolution was organized in Washington, DC.

The 1890-1891 Sioux Indian War was fought at Wounded Knee, SD.

The first electrocution took place at Auburn Prison in New York.

Sitting Bull, the chief of the Sioux Indians, was killed in North Dakota.

The Oklahoma Territory was created by an act of Congress.

science & technology

The pneumatic hammer was patented.

James B. Duke formed the American Tobacco Company in Durham, NC.

The American whaling industry began on the Pacific coast.

The United Mine Workers organized in Columbus, OH.

Steward Halstead introduced the use of rubber gloves in surgery.

religion

The Mormon Church in Salt Lake City discontinued its sanction of polygamy.

The hymns "Tenderly Calling" and "Tell Mother I'll Be There" were published.

arts & culture

Rudyard Kipling's works first appeared in the U.S.

J.A. Riis published his book *How the Other Half Lives*, which introduced the phrase into common usage.

The General Federation of Women's Clubs was formed.

The first Army-Navy football game was played at West Point, NY.

1891

politics

Congress created the Circuit Court of Appeals.

Congress passed the International Copyright Act, protecting foreign authors' rights.

U.S. sailors were injured in Valparaiso, Chile, by street mobs.

Robert Womack discovered gold at Cripple Creek, CO.

The Pre-emption Law was repealed. The Pre-emption Acts offered temporary protection of "Squatters rights" during the early phase of western settlement.

Robert E. Peary was sent to explore northern Greenland.

Texas established a railroad commission.

From 1866 to 1891, the U.S. Army fought 1,065 engagements with Indians across an area twice as large as the Civil War theater.

In Oklahoma, 900,000 acres of Indian land were opened for general settlement.

science & technology

W.L. Judson patented the zipper.

J.T. Smith patented corkboard.

The first important radio patent was issued to Thomas Edison.

Dynamite was exploded to produce artificial rain near Midland, TX.

T.A. Sperry originated trading stamps.

Carborundum was discovered.

Thomas Edison filed the first patent in the U.S. for the motion picture camera.

arts & culture

George M. Cohan made his first stage appearance at the age of 13.

Carnegie Hall opened in New York City with concerts conducted by Tchaikovsky.

The first correspondence school in the U.S. opened.

The first traveler's checks were devised by M.F. Berry.

The first international bicycle race in the U.S. was held at Madison Square Garden in New York.

Bob Fitzsimmons was the first U.S. Boxer to hold three titles: middle-, light- and heavyweight.

Y.M.C.A. instructor J. Naismith devised the game of basketball in Massachusetts.

1892

politics

Ellis Island in New York harbor became a receiving station for immigrants.

Illinois was the first state to make Lincoln's birthday a legal holiday.

Niagara Falls, NY was established.

The Dalton Gang was annihilated by a marshal's posse at Coffeyville, KS.

The U.S. launched the *Texas*, its first armored battleship.

William McKinley was elected governor of Ohio.

William Taft was a U.S. circuit judge at this time.

In Montana, 1.8 million acres of the Crow Indian Reservation were opened to settlers.

science & technology

The American Psychological Association was formed.

The first college of osteopathy in the U.S. was established at Kirkville, MO.

George Ferris designed the first ferris wheel.

The General Electric Co. was formed.

Dr. Sheldon Jackson introduced Siberian reindeer into Alaska.

T.L. Wilson of Spray, NC first manufactured acetylene.

The first cattle tuberculosis tests were performed in Villanova, PA.

The first gasoline powered automobile in the U.S. was made by C. and F. Duryea in Massachusetts.

The cork bottle-cap was invented.

The first moving picture "studio" was built in West Orange, NJ.

The first case of cholera was brought to New York by the *Hamburg-American* liner.

arts & culture

The songs "After the Ball" and "Bicycle Built for Two" were published.

The Adventures of Sherlock Holmes first appeared in the U.S.

The "diamond horseshoe" was first used to describe the boxes at the Metropolitan Opera House.

The first use of a pinch hitter in baseball occurred at Brooklyn, NY.

1893

politics

Grover Cleveland was inaugurated as the twenty-fourth president. (He was also the twenty-second.) Adlai Stevenson was his vice president.

A revolution in Hawaii deposed Queen Liliuokalani and a provisional government was formed.

The first Chinese were deported from San Francisco under the Chinese Exclusion Act.

The Cherokee Strip, 6 million acres between Kansas and Oklahoma, was opened for settlers.

President Cleveland opened the Columbian Exposition in Chicago.

The first foreign minister designated as an ambassador was sent to England.

The U.S. suffered a financial panic from 1893 to 1896.

Almost 500 banks failed during the year.

A total of $156,906,637.00 was paid out in government pensions.

The U.S. Mint building at Carson City, NV was also used as the U.S. Assay Office.

U.S. troops were ordered to withdraw from the Hawaiian Islands.

There were now 170,607 miles of railroad track in the U.S.

The national debt at this time was $1,556,281,905.00.

science & technology

The American Railway Union was organized in Chicago.

The U.S. Cruiser *Columbia* set a new speed record of 25 knots per hour.

The motion picture machine was invented by Thomas Edison.

Shredded Wheat was patented.

religion

The Mormon Temple was dedicated in Salt Lake City.

The Waldensians, a religious group from the French Alps, founded Valdese, NC.

arts & culture

Dr. Jekyll and Mr. Hyde by Robert Louis Stevenson was published in the U.S.

The "hootchy kootchy" dance, later called the shimmy, originated.

Lionel Barrymore made his stage debut in Philadelphia.

Over 2,000 people were killed in a cyclone along the Gulf Coast of Louisiana.

The Anti-Saloon League was founded in Oberlin, OH.

The first 18-hole golf course opened at Wheaton, IL.

1894

politics

Congress designated the first Monday in September as Labor Day and made it a legal holiday.

"Coxey's Army" marched from Ohio to Washington, DC to demonstrate for emergency aid to the unemployed.

The Hawaiian Republic was officially recognized by the U.S.

President Cleveland ordered federal troops to Chicago during a railroad strike.

Kelly's "hobo army," 1,200 strong, left San Francisco for Washington, DC and seized a railroad train on the way.

The federal government took over the printing of postage stamps from private companies.

New York became the first state to pass a dog license law.

The federal government issued $50 million in bonds to make up for gold losses.

science & technology

J.P. Morgan organized the Southern Railroad Co.

The first carbide factory was established in Spray, NC.

J.H. Bolles became the first woman osteopathic doctor.

The first electric engine was used on a railroad in Baltimore, MD.

D.M. Cooper patented the first time card recorder in Rochester, NY.

Thomas Edison exhibited his motion picture machine on Broadway in New York City.

arts & culture

Mark Twain made a world lecture tour.

Ethel Barrymore made her stage debut in New York at the age of 15.

Oliver Wendell Holmes, who was a physician, poet and essayist, died in Boston.

The first poliomyelitis epidemic broke out in Vermont.

The U.S. Golf Association was formed.

Yale's baseball team first employed the squeeze play.

1895

politics

A revolt against Spanish rule broke out in Cuba, beginning the Cuban revolution for independence.

The U.S. Post Office established rural free delivery (R.F.D.).

The militia was called out in the Brooklyn trolley strike.

The Bannock Indian disturbances occurred in what is now Idaho.

Pensacola, FL was established.

The Kickapoo run was made in Oklahoma.

The estimated national wealth of the U.S. was $77 billion.

Congress passed an income tax law that was declared unconstitutional by the Supreme Court.

science & technology

George Westinghouse constructed huge power generators at Niagara Falls, NY.

The first auto made for sale was produced by the Duryea Motor Wagon Company.

K.C. Gillette invented disposable razor blades.

Chiropractics was founded by Daniel D. Palmer in Davenport, IA.

Boston installed the first subway in America.

Large corporate salmon canneries opened in Alaska in the 1890s.

Milk was first pasteurized commercially.

Health insurance began to be sold in the U.S. in the 1890s.

The first tung trees were planted in Chico, CA.

The first pneumatic tire for the automobile was manufactured in Hartford, CT.

The first air-conditioned factory opened in Gastonia, NY.

The first meeting of the National Association of Manufacturers was held in Cincinnati, OH.

arts & culture

Player pianos came into the market.

The opera *Hansel und Gretel* was produced for the first time in the U.S. in New York City.

The songs "The Band Played On" and "There'll Come a Time" were published.

The American Bowling Congress was formed at Beethoven Hall, NY.

The first automobile race in the U.S. was run in Chicago, with records speeds of 7.5 miles per hour.

The first cafeteria opened in Chicago.

1896

politics	*science & technology*	*religion*	*arts & culture*

politics

Utah was admitted as the forty-fifth state.

Over 100,000 people headed for the gold discovered in the Klondike region of the Yukon in Canada.

Absentee voting was first permitted in the U.S. in Vermont.

The Jim Crow Law of Louisiana, which legalized racial segregation in public places, was declared unconstitutional by the Supreme Court.

At this time, seven-eighths of America's wealth was controlled by one-eighth of the population.

The first health ordinance prohibiting spitting was enacted in New York City.

science & technology

The first portable carousel was manufactured in Abilene, TX.

S.H. Kress & Co. was established in Memphis, TN.

The first flashlight was manufactured in New York City.

Radioactivity was discovered by Lord Rutherford.

The first automobile appeared in Detroit, MI.

H.L. Smith took the first X-ray photograph in Davidson, NC.

The first offshore oil wells were successfully drilled near Summerland, CA.

W.S. Hadaway patented the first electric stove.

H. Hubbell patented the electric light socket with pull chain.

religion

W.A. (Billy) Sunday, a professional baseball player and Y.M.C.A. secretary, began his career as an evangelist.

arts & culture

T.A. Metz wrote "There'll be a Hot Time in the Old Town Tonight."

The songs "Love Makes the World Go 'Round" and "Sweet Rosie O'Grady" were published.

Vaudeville theaters began showing motion pictures as a novelty.

A tornado in St. Louis killed 400 people.

Frank Broaker became the first certified public accountant in the U.S.

Americans won nine of twelve events in the first modern Olympic Games in Athens, Greece.

Dorothy Dix began her personal advice column in a New Orleans paper.

The first automobile accident occurred in New York City.

1897

politics

William McKinley was inaugurated as the twenty-fifth president. Garret A. Hobart was his vice president.

The first large shipments of Klondike gold arrived in San Francisco and Seattle.

The U.S. Distributed $50,000.00 in relief to destitute Cubans.

Prohibition of sales of intoxicating drinks to Indians was approved.

The Library of Congress was moved from the Capitol Building to its own building.

The Bering Sea Seal Treaty was signed, thus protecting the Pribilof Islands' seal herd by limiting hunting by Canadian, Russian and Japanese boats.

New postal laws provided for indemnity for the loss of registered mail.

U.S. submarines *Plunder* and *Argonaut* were tested successfully in Baltimore.

Apache Chief Geronimo and his band were held as prisoners of war at Fort Sill, OK from 1897 to 1912.

The Anglo-American Arbitration Treaty was signed.

Fire destroyed the state capitol building at Harrisburg, PA.

A total of 230,832 immigrants arrived in the U.S.

Theodore Roosevelt was named Assistant Secretary of the Navy.

The Bitterroot National Forest was established in Montana.

The national debt at this time was $1,808,777,643.00.

science & technology

The American Osteopathic Association was formed.

The first shipment of fresh halibut was sent south from Juneau, AK.

C.W. Post introduced breakfast cereal.

The American Forestry Association was incorporated.

The first rock wool factory opened in Alexandria, IN.

arts & culture

John Philip Sousa published "Stars and Stripes Forever."

W.W. Price became the first White House news correspondent.

S.S. Kresge variety stores were founded.

The ice cream sundae originated in Utica, NY.

The central states were hit by an earthquake.

James J. Corbett beat Robert Fitzsimmons in the first boxing match to be filmed by a movie camera.

Rudolph Dirks began writing the first American comic strip, *Katzenjammer Kids*.

1898

politics

The American battleship *Maine* was blown up in Havana Harbor.

The Spanish-American War began.

President McKinley issued a call for volunteers for the military.

Colonel Leonard Wood and Lieutenant Colonel Theodore Roosevelt organized the "Rough-Riders," the first U.S. Volunteer Cavalry Regiment.

"Remember the *Maine*," in reference to the American naval ship sunk by the Spanish, became the American battle cry.

U.S. Marines repulsed Spanish forces in battle at Guantanamo Bay, Cuba.

The Pacific island of Guam surrendered to the U.S.

The Hawaiian Islands, 6,740 square miles, were annexed by the U.S.

Americans took El Caney and San Juan, Cuba.

Spanish General Toral surrendered Santiago and 24,000 Spanish troops to American General Shaffer.

The Spanish government formally accepted U.S. peace terms.

There were 5,462 American casualties during the war. Over 90% of those were caused by disease. Fewer than 400 American soldiers were killed in battle.

The U.S. took possession of Puerto Rico (3,435 square miles) and the Philippine Islands (114,958 square miles).

The U.S. acquired the Pine Islands in the West Indies (882 square miles).

The Chippewa Indian disturbances occurred.

The Nome, AK gold rush began.

Wake Island was acquired by the U.S.

The Peary Arctic Club was formed in New York to find the North Pole.

The first Spanish contract laborers arrived in Hawaii.

The U.S. became an important world power by securing new lands.

science & technology

Atlantic City, NJ opened the first steel pier.

The first automobile advertisement and the first auto insurance first appeared in Hartford, CT.

The first automobile truck was designed.

arts & culture

Henry James published his gothic novella, *The Turn of the Screw*.

1899

politics

President McKinley signed a peace treaty with Spain.

Cuba came under the sovereignty of the U.S.

The U.S. acquired the Samoan Islands (77 square miles).

General MacArthur (the father of General Douglas MacArthur) occupied Luzon Island in the Philippines.

The first experimental U.S. mail collection was made in Cleveland, OH. The Post Office did not set up a vehicle division for 15 years.

Congress authorized voting machines.

Czar Nicholas II of Russia called the first Hague Peace Conference.

Congress established Mount Rainier National Park in Washington.

The Philippine Insurrection occurred, lasting until 1902.

Martha Place, in Sing Sing Prison, NY was the first woman to go to the electric chair.

Theodore Roosevelt was the governor of New York at this time.

Gold was discovered near where Fairbanks, AK now stands.

From 1850 to 1900, 250,000 miles of railroad track were laid in the U.S.

science & technology

The first motor-driven vacuum cleaner was patented.

The first golf tee was patented in Boston.

H. O'Sullivan patented the first rubber heel in Lowell, MA.

R.E. Olds built the first automobile factory in Detroit, MI.

arts & culture

Theodore Dreiser wrote *Sister Carrie*.

The "Cake Walk" became the fashionable dance.

The songs "Always," "My Wild Irish Rose," and "Where the Sweet Magnolias Grow" were published.

George M. Cohan and his family were performing on Broadway at this time.

Elbert Hubbard published *The Message to Garcia*.

President McKinley was the first president to ride in an automobile.

H.H. Bliss of New York City became the first automobile fatality in the U.S.

An epidemic of bubonic plague began in Honolulu, HI.

The practice of tarring and feathering for punishment, which was never legal, disappeared in the latter part of the nineteenth century.

1900

politics

The population of the U.S. at this time was 75,994,575.

The estimated national wealth at this time was $88,517,306,775.00.

At this time, 185,000 people were served by Rural Free Delivery. By 1924, 6.5 million would be served.

President McKinley appointed S.B. Dole the first governor of Hawaii.

A race riot broke out in Akron, OH.

William H. Taft was appointed to help form a civil government in the Philippines.

President McKinley signed the Gold Standard Currency Bill.

Robert E. Peary attempted to discover the North Pole.

The U.S. State Department negotiated to purchase the Virgin Islands. THe sale was not completed until 1917.

The state capitol building of Colorado, with its golden dome, was completed.

The new state capitol building of New Mexico was dedicated.

science & technology

Andrew Carnegie and J.D. Rockefeller began making contributions to various organizations.

The first chiropractic school opened in Davenport, IA.

The Santa Fe Railroad, running from Chicago to San Francisco was completed.

The first escalator was manufactured in New York City.

religion

A survey of religious affiliations in the U.S. revealed that there were 6 million Methodists, 5 million Baptists, 1.5 million Lutherans, 1.5 million Presbyterians, 350,000 Mormons and 80,000 Christian Scientists.

arts & culture

Ragtime jazz developed in the U.S.

Engineer Casey Jones died at the throttle of the Cannonball.

At this time there were 8,000 automobiles in the U.S. and less than 10 miles of concrete pavement.

There were 1,335,911 telephones in use in the U.S. this year.

The Associated Press news agency was founded in New York.

The Hall of Fame was formed by New York University, and the first *Who's Who in America* was issued.

The first 4-H club was formed in Illinois.

A hurricane killed 6,000 people in Galveston, TX.

1901

politics

President McKinley was inaugurated for his second term. Theodore Roosevelt was his vice president.

The Pan-American Exposition opened in Buffalo, NY.

President McKinley was shot in Buffalo, NY. He died later of his wound at the age of 58.

Theodore Roosevelt was sworn in as the twenty-sixth president in Buffalo, NY.

The Army Nurse Corps was organized as a branch of the U.S. Army.

Congress created the U.S. Army Dental Corps.

New York was the first state to require auto license plates.

The Kiowa-Comanche lands in the Oklahoma Territory were opened for settlement.

The Carlsbad Caverns in New Mexico were discovered by cowboy Jim White.

The New York State Board of Health condemned Sing Sing Prison.

The Cuban constitution was signed.

Carrie Nation was arrested for wrecking saloons in Kansas.

The Port Orchard Naval Station in Washington was enlarged and became the Puget Sound Navy Yard.

William Taft became the first civil governor of the Philippines.

Benjamin Harrison died at the age of 67 and was buried in Indianapolis, IN.

The Army War College was organized.

The new state house in Providence, RI was completed.

Shortly after becoming president, Teddy Roosevelt spoke his famous words, "Speak softly and carry a big stick."

science & technology

Proof was presented for the first time that yellow fever was transmitted by mosquitos.

The first motorcycle with a built-in gas engine was manufactured in Springfield, MA.

About 4,000 automobiles were manufactured this year.

Karl Landersteiner discovered the different human blood types.

The Spindletop oil well near Beaumont, TX, brought the oil industry to Texas.

A.C. Bostwick was the first to drive an auto at a speed of more than a mile a minute.

1902

politics

The U.S. Army's traditional blue uniforms were changed to olive drab.

The permanent Bureau of the Census office was established.

The Cuban Republic was inaugurated.

The U.S. Army was reduced to 66,497 men.

The U.S. flag was lowered from government buildings in Cuba and replaced with the Cuban flag.

The Panama Canal property was offered to the U.S. for $40 million.

The U.S. offered relief aid to the people of St. Pierre, Martinique after the eruption of Mt. Pelee.

Robert E. Peary made a second attempt to reach the North Pole.

Maryland passed the first working men's state compensation law.

Woodrow Wilson was named the president of Princeton University.

The Reclamation Act was passed by Congress.

West Point was to be rebuilt at a cost of $6 million.

science & technology

The International Harvester Company was incorporated in New Jersey.

The average wage of shopgirls in Boston was between $5.00 and $6.00 per week.

The first wireless message was sent across the Atlantic Ocean.

The laying of a Pacific cable was begun in San Francisco.

Window envelopes were patented.

The first cancer research fund was established in New York City.

Train fare to California from the East Coast ranged from $30.00 to $50.00 depending on the starting point.

arts & culture

Henry James published *The Ambassadors*.

The songs "Bill Bailey, Won't You Please Come Home," "In The Good Old Summertime" and "Pomp and Circumstance" were published.

The Virginian by Owen Wister was published. It later sold over a million copies.

T.J. Talley opened a theater in Los Angeles exclusively for motion pictures.

The first post-season bowl football game was held in Pasadena, CA.

1903

politics

Wisconsin was the first state to adopt mandatory primary elections.

The Hay-Bunan-Varilla Treaty was negotiated, giving the U.S. control of the Panama Canal.

New Hampshire authorized liquor sales after 48 years of prohibition.

The Department of Commerce and Labor was created.

The Bureau of Standards was placed under the Department of Commerce and Labor.

President Roosevelt designated Pelican Island near Florida as the first wildlife refuge.

The Pacific cable opened, and President Roosevelt sent a message around the world in 12 minutes.

The Louisiana Purchase Exposition Buildings in St. Louis were dedicated.

The Republic of Panama was proclaimed.

The boundary between the U.S. and Canada was fixed at its present location.

The National Guard was given formal status as an organized militia.

New York became the first state to take fingerprints in a state prison.

science & technology

Wilbur and Orville Wright made their famous flight.

Henry Ford organized and became the president of the Ford Motor Co.

The first steel passenger railroad coach was completed in Altoona, PA.

arts & culture

Enrico Caruso, the famous Italian tenor, made his U.S. debut at the Metropolitan Opera.

John Barrymore made his stage debut at the Cleveland Theatre in Chicago.

Tin Pan Alley in New York, where many songs originated, became well known.

The Great Train Robbery was the first motion picture with a real plot.

The songs "Sweet Adeline," "Ida! Sweet as Apple Cider" and "Toyland" were published.

The first female ushers were employed at the Majestic Theatre in New York City.

The Jamaica Rack Track opened at Long Island, NY.

The first transcontinental auto trip from San Francisco to New York City was completed.

1904

politics

The St. Louis Exposition celebrated the centennial of the Louisiana Purchase.

A total of 812,870 immigrants arrived in the U.S.

New York City first began using mounted police.

The U.S. formally acquired the Panama Canal Zone.

William Taft was named Secretary of War.

The U.S. declared its neutrality in the Russo-Japanese War.

President Roosevelt sent William Taft to Panama to reassure its citizens.

The U.S. established its third mint in Denver, CO.

The first speed laws in the U.S. were established in New York. They were 20 miles per hour in the open country, 15 in villages and 10 in urban areas.

The national debt at this time was $2,264,003,585.00.

science & technology

The first exhibition of a diesel engine in the U.S. occurred at the St. Louis Exposition.

The Bethlehem Steel Corporation was founded.

The American Tobacco Company was formed.

The New York City subway opened.

The National Tuberculosis Association was formed in Atlantic City, NJ.

The Fuller office building, nicknamed the "Flatiron Building" because of its shape, was completed in New York City. At 22 stories, standing at 280 feet, it was the tallest building in the world.

H.D. Week patented the automobile tire chain.

The first installment finance company was organized in Rochester, NY.

arts & culture

Henry James published *The Golden Bowl*.

O'Henry's collection of short stories, *Cabbages and Kings*, was published.

Victor Herbert's operetta *Mlle. Modiste* opened in New York.

The songs "Give My Regards to Broadway" and "Meet Me in St. Louis" were published.

The first Olympic Games in America were held at the St. Louis Exposition.

The sea wall at Galveston, TX was completed.

The awarding of the Rhodes scholarships began in the U.S.

The first ice cream cones were introduced at the St. Louis Exposition.

A policemen in New York arrested a woman for smoking in public.

1905

politics

Theodore Roosevelt was inaugurated for his second term as president. Charles W. Fairbanks was his vice president.

Russia and Japan accepted President Roosevelt's proposal for a peace parley.

The Executive Mansion became knows as the White House during Roosevelt's administration.

Robert E. Peary sailed from New York for the North Pole.

New York began an investigation into life insurance companies.

A total of $141,142,861.00 was paid out in government pensions.

A total of 1,027,421 immigrants arrived in the U.S.

science &
technology

The first commercial production of Douglas fir plywood began in St. Johns, OR.

Electric lamps were put in railroad cars for the first time in Chicago.

Glass paving-bricks were announced, but never came into use.

The first large oil field in Oklahoma opened near Tulsa.

Fingerprinting began to be used in law enforcement.

The Great Western Sugar Company was incorporated.

Helium was discovered as a natural gas constituent.

The Mount Wilson observatory was completed in California.

arts &
culture

Edith Wharton's first novel, *House of Mirth*, was published.

Victor Herbert's operetta *The Red Mill* opened in New York.

The weekly journal *Variety* was founded.

Will Rogers began his stage career in the New York Theater.

Library book wagons (traveling libraries) began to be used.

The songs "Claire de Lune," "In My Merry Oldsmobile" and "In the Shade of the Old Apple Tree" were published.

The number of automobiles in the U.S. rose to 77,988.

The first rotary club was founded by Paul Percy Harris, a Chicago lawyer.

Before the government anti-mosquito campaign, 400 people died in New Orleans of yellow fever.

New York defeated Philadelphia in the World Series.

The Staten Island Ferry began service in New York.

1906

politics

President Roosevelt personally inspected the Panama Canal. It was the first time a president left the country while in office.

President Roosevelt declared Devil's Tower, WY as the first national monument.

A total of 1,100,725 immigrants arrived in the U.S.

Congress chartered the National Education Association.

Congress passed the Pure Food and Drug Act, the first major legislation regulating the preparation of food and patent medicines.

Robert E. Peary made his third attempt to discover the North Pole.

President Palma of Cuba and his cabinet resigned, and American control was established.

President Roosevelt received the Nobel Peace Prize for his efforts in ending the Russo-Japanese War.

Congress passed the Meat Inspection Act.

The S.O.S. radio distress signal was adopted.

A total of $139,000,288.00 was paid out in government pensions.

science & technology

The Norfolk and Southern Railway was organized.

Dr. Lee DeForest invented the three-electrode vacuum tube (the radio).

The Pennsylvania Railroad announced that all cars would henceforth be made of steel instead of wood.

religion

The first Church of Christ was dedicated in Boston.

arts & culture

Upton Sinclair's *The Jungle* was published.

The Four Million, a collection of short stories by O'Henry, was published.

The first known radio program of voice and music was broadcast in the U.S.

Zane Grey published his first successful book, *The Spirit of the Border*.

The first motion picture animated cartoon was released.

The songs "Anchors Aweigh," "I Love You Truly," "In Old New York" and "You're a Grand Old Flag" were published.

A devastating earthquake hit San Francisco, causing a huge fire.

President Roosevelt's daughter Alice was married in the White House.

President Roosevelt made the phrase "square deal" popular.

Picture hats with ostrich plumes were the latest in feminine headgear.

1907

politics

The Oklahoma Territory and the Indian Territory were joined to form the state of Oklahoma, which became the forty-sixth state.

President Roosevelt appointed the Inland Waterways Commission.

The second Hague Peace Conference was held at the suggestion of President Roosevelt. The U.S. advocated the formation of a world court.

The U.S. fiscal year closed with a surplus of $87 million.

Congress passed a law excluding Japanese from the U.S. except under passport.

The U.S. had its twentieth economic depression since 1790.

Immigration reached an all-time high, with 1,285,349 foreigners arriving in the U.S.: 116,000 from Great Britain, 285,000 from Germany, and 258,000 from Italy.

President Roosevelt sent the "great white fleet" of 16 battleships around the world.

Calvin Coolidge was elected to the Massachusetts House of Representatives.

science & technology

The first fleet of taxi-meter cabs arrived in New York from Paris.

The Cape Cod Canal was begun.

arts & culture

Franz Lehar's production *The Merry Widow* introduced the popular songs "I Love You So," "Vilia" and "The Merry Widow Waltz."

The songs "Glow Worm," "On the Road to Mandalay," "School Days" and "Red Wing" were published.

The first Ziegfeld Follies was staged in New York.

Mother's Day was first observed in Philadelphia.

A fire at Coney Island, NY caused $1.5 million in damage.

Chicago defeated Detroit in the World Series.

The steamer *Larchmont* floundered in the Long Island Sound, causing 131 deaths.

Christmas seals were first sold in America by the Red Cross secretary.

The United Press was formed by E.W. Scripps and M.A. McRoe.

The first municipal stadium was completed by San Francisco.

Mine explosions in West Virginia and Pennsylvania caused 600 deaths.

Perforations and embroidery made "peek-a-boo" shirtwaists for ladies.

1908

politics

The Federal Bureau of Investigation (FBI) was established under the Justice Department.

Lyndon B. Johnson was born near Stonewall, TX.

The U.S. Navy established the Nurse Corps.

A total of 783,870 immigrants arrived in the U.S.

Smoking by women in public places was made illegal in New York City.

The American Battleship fleet nearly circumnavigated the globe.

The city manager plan of municipal government originated in Staunton, VA.

The National Monetary Commission was appointed to regulate banking and currency.

The Navy Department dredged an entrance channel 600 feet wide at Pearl Harbor.

Robert E. Peary began his fourth attempt to find the North Pole.

A total of $153,093,086.00 was paid out in government pensions.

science & technology

The Singer building, at 47 stories, was the first great skyscraper in New York City.

The East River Tunnel from the Battery in Manhattan to Brooklyn, NY was opened.

The General Motors Co. was organized by W.C. Durant of Flint, MI.

The first person was killed in a plane accident while flying with Orville Wright.

Over 50,000 autos were manufactured. The new style of auto had a glass-enclosed body.

The first credit union association was founded in Manchester, NH.

The Ford Motor Co. introduced the Model T, priced at $850.00.

religion

The New England Methodist Conference removed its bans on dancing, card playing and theater attendance.

The first Gideon Bible was placed in Superior Hotel in Iron Mountain, MT.

arts & culture

The Dixieland Jazz Band was formed in New Orleans.

Gertrude Stein's *Three Lives* was published.

Chicago defeated Detroit in the World Series.

1909

politics

William Howard Taft was inaugurated as the twenty-seventh president. James S. Sherman was his vice president.

The National Association for the Advancement of Colored People (NAACP) was founded.

The Lincoln-head penny, issued by the Philadelphia mint, replaced the Indian-head penny.

Apache Indian Chief Geronimo died on an Oklahoma reservation.

A total of 751,786 immigrants arrived in the U.S.

Thousands of acres of land were opened for settlement in Montana, Washington and Idaho.

The Alaska, Yukon, Pacific Exposition opened in Seattle, WA.

The first junior high school was authorized in Berkeley, CA.

A total of $161,973,703.00 was paid out in government pensions.

science & technology

The first production of Bakelite advanced the plastic industry.

The Queensboro and Manhattan Bridges were both opened for traffic in New York City.

Ole Evinrude developed the outboard motor in Milwaukee, WI.

The DeVilbiss Company manufactured a spray-painting device in Toledo, OH.

arts & culture

Irish tenor John McCormack popularized "Mother Machree" and "When Irish Eyes Are Smiling" in America.

The songs "By the Light of the Silvery Moon," "I Wonder Who's Kissing Her Now," "Meet Me Tonight in Dream-Land," "Put on Your Old Grey Bonnet" and "The Wiffenpoof Song" were popular at this time.

S. McCay created the first notable animated cartoon, *Gertie and the Dinosaur*.

Pittsburgh defeated Detroit in the World Series.

The latest creation in feminine fashion was the hobble skirt.

The Indianapolis Motor Speedway was built between 1909 and 1910.

1910

politics

The population of the 46 states at this time was 91,972,266.

Postal Savings was established.

Illiteracy in America reached a new low of 7.7% of the population.

A total of 1,041,570 immigrants arrived in the U.S.

The estimated national wealth of the U.S. at this time was $220 billion.

Congress passed the Mann Act, which restricted the transporting of minor women across state borders.

The Pan-American Union of 21 republics in the western hemisphere met in Buenos Aires.

The U.S. Bureau of Mines was established.

Glacier National Park in Montana was established.

Race riots took place in Illinois and Texas.

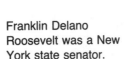

Franklin Delano Roosevelt was a New York state senator.

The national debt at this time was $2,704,142,281.00.

science & technology

Eugene Ely made the first plane take off from a U.S. warship.

The first photostat copying machine was manufactured in Rochester, NY.

Columbia University established the first optics and optometry course in New York City.

Halley's Comet appeared.

A.F. Knight patented the first steel shaft for golf clubs.

arts & culture

Charlie Chaplin at this time was a minor British comedian appearing in a vaudeville act called Karno's Wow-Wows.

Victor Herbert's *Naughty Marietta* opened in New York.

The songs "Ah! Sweet Mystery of Life," "Down By the Old Mill Stream" and "Let Me Call You Sweetheart" were published.

Mark Twain died at the age of 75.

The Boy Scouts of America was incorporated.

Philadelphia defeated Chicago in the World Series.

Pennsylvania Station was built in New York City.

Most women carried sunshades at this time.

1911

politics

President Taft ordered 20,000 U.S. troops to the Mexican border.

The U.S. Army opened its pilot training schools.

The U.S. Supreme Court ordered Standard Oil Co. and the American Tobacco Co. to be dissolved, charging that they were monopolies.

A total of 878,587 immigrants arrived in the U.S.

The government opened experimental postal saving banks in every state and territory.

Woodrow Wilson was elected Governor of New Jersey.

A total of $157,325,160.00 was paid out in government pensions.

The state capitol building of Missouri and New York burned.

Robert E. Peary was given the rank of Rear Admiral for discovering the North Pole.

The U.S., Canada and Japan agreed to ban seal fishing in the Bering Sea and north of the 30th parallel.

science & technology

The Roosevelt Dam on the Salt River in Arizona was completed.

John D. Rockefeller resigned as president of Standard Oil.

Over half of all industrial workers in the U.S. were of foreign birth at this time.

U.S. coal production was over 500 million tons a year.

C.F. Kettering of Dayton, OH invented the automobile self-starter.

arts & culture

Edith Wharton published *Ethan Frome*.

The songs "Alexander's Ragtime Band," "Good Night Ladies," "Oh You Beautiful Doll" and "I Want a Girl Just Like the Girl that Married Dear Old Dad" were published.

The first motion pictures were being made in Hollywood, CA.

"Little Theater" groups began forming across the country.

The first cross-country airplane flight was made by Calbraith P. Rogers.

Philadelphia defeated New York in the World Series.

The first pilot's license was issued by the Aero Club of America.

1912

politics

New Mexico became the forty-seventh state.

Arizona became the forty-eighth state.

The parcel post system was authorized to begin on January 1, 1913.

Theodore Roosevelt was shot while giving a speech, but continued the speech until he had finished.

An 8-hour day labor law was extended to all workers under federal contract.

New York passed a 54-hour week labor law.

Theodore Roosevelt announced, "My hat is in the ring," declaring his candidacy for president.

Government regulation of radio began.

The Bull Moose Party seceded from the Republican Party and nominated Theodore Roosevelt for president.

Limited territorial status was granted to Alaska.

The Chamber of Commerce of the United States was established.

A total of 838,172 immigrants arrived in the U.S.

The Marines reopened telegraph communications between the U.S. and Nicaragua.

Massachusetts became the first state to establish a minimum wage for women and children.

A total of $152,986,433.00 was paid out in government pensions.

science & technology

Isaac N. Lewis invented the machine gun.

arts & culture

The songs "Waiting for the Robert E. Lee," "The Sweetheart of Sigma Chi," "Moonlight Bay" and "It's a Long, Long Way to Tipperary" were published.

The oceanliner *Titanic* struck an iceberg and sank, killing 1,595 people.

The Girl Scouts of America was founded in Savannah, GA.

James Thorpe, an American Indian, was proclaimed the world's greatest athlete.

Boston defeated New York in the World Series.

The first recorded self-service grocery store opened in Pomona, CA.

1913

politics

Woodrow Wilson was inaugurated as the twenty-eighth president. Thomas R. Marshall was his vice president.

Richard M. Nixon was born in Yorba Linda, CA.

Gerald R. Ford was born in Omaha, NE.

The Sixteenth Amendment was adopted, allowing the federal government to levy and collect taxes without apportionment to the state.

The Seventeenth Amendment was adopted, allowing for popular election of U.S. senators. Previously,they had been appointed by state legislatures.

The U.S. suffered an economic depression.

The Alamo in San Antonio, TX was restored to its original form.

The Federal Reserve System was established.

The U.S. had 26,664 banks at this time.

The Panama Canal was completed.

A total of 1,197,892 immigrants arrived in the U.S.

F.D. Roosevelt was named Assistant Secretary of the Navy.

The Department of Labor was detached from the Department of Commerce.

The U.S. Board of Mediation and Conciliation was established to settle labor disputes and strikes.

The Veterans of Foreign Wars of the U.S. was organized.

A huge reunion of Civil War veterans was held at Gettysburg.

A total of $174,171,660.00 was paid out in government pensions.

science & technology

Henry Ford set up his first assembly line and raised wages to $5.00 a day.

The first drive-in car service station was opened in Pittsburgh. PA.,

arts & culture

Willa Cather published *O Pioneers!*

Edith Wharton's *The Custom of the Country* was published.

The "Foxtrot" came into fashion.

Irene and Vernon Castle made their American debut in *The Sunshine Girl*.

The songs "Danny Boy" and "Peg O' My Heart" were published.

Philadelphia defeated New York in the World Series.

The first crossword puzzle was published.

Mother's Day was first observed nationally.

1914

politics

The Panama Canal was formally opened and the Panama Canal Zone was established.

Mexico severed diplomatic relations with the U.S.

President Wilson ordered the American fleet to Tampico Bay, Mexico.

The Federal Trade Commission was established.

Congress authorized the Alaska Railroad.

Ground was broken in Washington, DC for the $2 million Lincoln Memorial.

The government quarantined many states for foot-and-mouth disease among cattle.

Herbert Hoover was the chairman of the American Relief Committee in London.

A total of 1,218,480 immigrants arrived in the U.S.

For the second time, J.S. Coxey led an army of the unemployed from Ohio to Washington, DC.

U.S. Marines landed in Haiti.

A total of $172,417,546.26 was paid in government pensions.

For the first time, citizens paid a federal income tax.

World War I erupted in Europe. President Wilson declared U.S. neutrality.

science & technology

The first traffic light was installed in Cleveland, OH.

The Cape Cod Canal was opened.

A tidal wave brought death and destruction to Galveston, TX

arts & culture

Penrod by Booth Tarkington was published.

Tarzan of the Apes by Edgar Rice Burroughs was published.

Joyce Kilmer's poem "Trees" was published.

The American Society of Composers and Publishers was organized.

The songs "By the Beautiful Sea," "St. Louis Blues" and "Missouri Waltz" were published.

The first road map was published in Pittsburgh, PA.

Boston defeated Philadelphia in the World Series.

Margaret Sanger was arrested for distributing a pamphlet on birth control called "Family Limitations."

President Wilson's first wife died in the White House.

1915

politics

The steamship *Lusitania* was sunk without warning; 1,198 lives were lost.

Congress established the U.S. Coast Guard by combining the Revenue Cutter Service and the Life Saving Service.

Nevada passed its "easy divorce" law.

The first warships passed through the Panama Canal.

The second Ku Klux Klan was formed.

Over 40,000 men paraded in Chicago protesting the closing of saloons on Sunday.

A total of 326,700 immigrants arrived in the U.S.

The estimated national wealth at this time was $228 billion.

Warren G. Harding was a U.S. senator at this time.

Herbert Hoover was named chairman of relief in Belgium.

Wireless communication was established between the U.S. and Japan.

science & technology

The one millionth automobile was produced by the Ford Plant in Detroit. Airplanes were first used to detect forest fires in Wisconsin.

The Victor Phonograph Company introduced the "Victrola," a record-playing machine.

Joseph Goldberger discovered that pellagra is a nutritional deficiency disease.

The first automobile finance company was organized in New York.

arts & culture

The film *Birth of a Nation* opened at Clune's Auditorium in Los Angeles.

Robert Frost was established as a major poet with the publication of "Boys Will" and "North of Boston."

The songs "The Old Grey Mare," "On the Beach at Waikiki," "Pack Up Your Troubles" and "Memories" were published.

Vice-President Marshall spoke the famous words, "What this country needs is a good 5¢ cigar."

Norman Tabor of the U.S. ran the mile in 4 minutes and 12.6 seconds.

President Wilson married Edith Bolling Galt.

Boston defeated Philadelphia in the World Series.

1916

politics

Mexican revolutionary leader Pancho Villa attacked Columbus, NM.

General John J. Pershing was ordered to Mexico to capture Pancho Villa.

The Senate voted to bring the Army to full strength.

President Wilson warned Germany to recall its U-boats.

The U.S. signed a treaty with Denmark to purchase the Danish West Indies for $25 million.

The National Park Service was established as a part of the Department of the Interior.

The Boy Scouts of America was incorporated in a bill signed by President Wilson.

A total of 298,826 immigrants arrived in the U.S.

The National Defense Act made the National Guard a part of the nation's military forces.

The Officer's Reserve Corps was established.

The first child labor law was enacted.

National Flag Day was proclaimed by President Wilson.

President Wilson won reelection on the slogan, "He kept us out of war."

The U.S. Marines landed in Nicaragua and the Dominican Republic.

The Army Veterinary Corps was established.

A total of $159,155,089.92 was paid out in government pensions.

science & technology

The submachine gun, or Tommy gun, was invented by Brigadier General J.T. Thompson.

Automobile production in the U.S. passed the one million per year mark. The average price of a new auto was $600.00.

arts & culture

Eugene O'Neill wrote *Bound East for Cardiff*.

Carl Sandburg's *Chicago Poems* was published.

Theodore Dreiser's *The Genius* was suppressed by New York censors.

The songs "I Ain't Got Nobody" and "Beale Street Blues" were published.

Silent movies were in their heyday and doing a large business.

Jack London, novelist and war correspondent, killed himself in Glen Ellen, CA.

Henrietta Howland Green, America's richest woman, died in New York, leaving a $100 million estate.

Margaret Sanger opened the first birth control clinic in Brooklyn, NY.

Boston defeated Brooklyn in the World Series.

1917

politics

President Wilson was inaugurated for his second term. Thomas R. Marshall was his vice-president.

The U.S. entered World War I.

The U.S. Senate adopted the "cloture rule," a procedure by which debate is ended and an immediate vote is taken.

John F. Kennedy was born in Brookline, MA.

Jeanette Rankin of Montana was the first woman member of the U.S. House of Representatives.

General Pershing was ordered home from Mexico after 11 unsuccessful months of looking for Pancho Villa.

Congress purchased the Virgin Islands and passed the Selective Service Bill.

U.S. troops began arriving in France.

The first excess profits tax was approved by Congress. The tax was enacted to capture for the federal government the extra profits made during wartime.

There were 4,842,139 motor vehicles registered in the U.S.

An aide to General Pershing spoke the famous words, "Lafayette, we are here!"

President Wilson, in a speech to congress, said, "The world must be safe for democracy."

The Mt. McKinley National Park was established in Alaska.

A total of 295,403 immigrants arrived in the U.S.

New York City was the largest city in the world, with a population of 5,737,492.

There was $4,924,928,348.00 in circulation in the U.S., or $47.03 per capita.

U.S. exports exceeded $6 billion for the year.

A total of $160,895,053.94 was paid out in government pensions.

The federal government began an investigation into the hygienic and safety standards of the meat-packing industry.

science & technology

Helium plants were erected in Texas.

The first two-way radios were installed in planes.

arts & culture

T.S. Eliot's *Prufrock and Other Observations* was published.

Upton Sinclair wrote *King Coal.*

Will Rogers joined the Ziegfeld Follies of 1917 as a rope twirler.

The songs "Over There," "The Bells of St. Mary's" and "For Me and My Gal" were published.

Chicago defeated New York in the World Series.

The International Association of Lions Clubs was formed.

Stylish young women began to bob their hair.

1918

politics

The wartime sugar ration was reduced to two pounds per person per month.

President Wilson named Bernard Baruch to take over the War Industries Board.

The federal registration of alien Germans began in the U.S.

The approximate cost of the first year of the war was $9 billion.

The first airmail stamps were issued.

The U.S. went on daylight saving time for the first time.

This was the first year that passports were required of foreigners, except for during the Civil War.

The Distinguished Service Medal was authorized.

The Wartime Prohibition Act was passed.

The Aisne-Marne offensive, in which 270,000 U.S. troops

and French units succeeded in establishing a battlefront from Soissons to Rheims, France, was the turning point of the war.

In the Meuse-Argonne Battle, 1.2 million American troops were deployed.

President Wilson announced the war aims and peace terms to Congress.

Germany offered to accept President Wilson's terms for peace.

Armistice was signed on November 11.

Kaiser Wilhelm II abdicated office in Germany.

President Wilson announced that he would attend the peace conference in person.

The number of U.S. forces involved in the war was 4,355,000.

The number of dead and wounded from the war was 364,800.

There were one million more women employees in 1918 than in 1915.

The American Railway Express Company was formed under federal supervision.

religion

Forty-five divided synods organized the United Lutheran Church.

arts & culture

Willa Cather's *My Antonia* was published.

The Magnificent Ambersons, by Booth Tarkington, was published.

Jerome Kern's *Rock-a-Bye Baby* opened in New York.

The songs "Hinky-Dinky Parlez-Vouz," "Hindustan," "I'm Always Chasing Rainbows" and "K-K-K-Katy" were published.

The first issue of the Army newspaper *Stars & Stripes* was published.

An influenza epidemic in 46 states caused over 400,000 deaths in the U.S.

Boxer Jack Dempsey knocked out Carl Morris in 14 seconds in New Orleans.

1919

politics

President Wilson presented a proposal for the formation of the League of Nations to the Peace Conference in Paris.

Congress ratified the Eighteenth Amendment prohibiting liquor traffic in the U.S.

The Treaty of Versailles, ending World War I, was signed, but was never ratified by the U.S. Senate.

The U.S. resumed trade with Germany.

President Wilson suffered a stroke.

A draft of the League of Nations plan was completed by the Allied Powers.

The drydock at Pearl Harbor, HI was completed.

As Governor of Massachusetts, Calvin Coolidge broke the Boston police strike.

The American Legion was founded in Paris and incorporated by Congress.

Over 2.4 million farms in the U.S. were operated by tenants.

The Yap Mandate put all German Pacific Island possessions north of the equator under Japanese control.

The first state gasoline tax was levied in Oregon.

Wisconsin was the first state to ratify the Nineteenth Amendment, granting women's suffrage.

Theodore Roosevelt died at the age of 61 in Oyster Bay, NY.

science & technology

During the year, nearly 4.1 million workers went on strike or were prevented from working by employers unsatisfied by workers' demands.

The Radio Corporation of America (RCA) was incorporated.

The pig iron output of the U.S. this year was 40 million tons.

arts & culture

Corn Huskers, a collection of poems by Carl Sandburg, was published.

Sherwood Anderson wrote *Winesburg, Ohio.*

The years 1919 to 1929 were known in the music world as the Jazz Age.

Andrew Carnegie died in Lenox, MA.

Jack Dempsey beat Jess Willard to become the world heavyweight champ.

Cincinnati defeated Chicago in the World Series.

Ladies' hemlines were now six inches off the ground.

1920

politics

The population of the 48 states at this time was 105,710,620.

The period of "Prohibition" began. Effected by the Eighteenth Amendment, it became illegal to manufacture, sell or transport liquor.

Life expectancy in the U.S. at this time was 54.09 years.

Airmail service began between New York and California.

The Merchant Marine Act was passed to encourage American shipping.

The War Department adopted shoulder insignia patches on Army uniforms.

The Ku Klux Klan began a period of large growth in the 1920s.

Fort Benning, GA was established as an infantry school.

The U.S. suffered its twenty-third economic depression since 1790.

Large meat-packing firms voluntarily agreed to federal demands that they sell their stockyards, railroads, warehouses and terminals to eliminate their monopolies.

The American Legion had 843,013 members in its first year.

The Nineteenth Amendment passed, granting women the right to vote.

The U.S. had 68 cities with populations of over 100,000.

For the first time in the history of the U.S. the country had a larger urban population than a rural population.

The national debt at this time was $24,299,321,467.00.

science & technology

Station KDKA in Pittsburgh, PA began the first radio broadcasting.

Over 1.9 million automobiles were manufactured during the year.

arts & culture

F. Scott Fitzgerald wrote *This Side of Paradise*.

Sinclair Lewis's *Main Street* was published.

Eugene O'Neill wrote the plays *The Emperor Jones* and *Beyond the Horizon*.

The Age of Innocence by Edith Wharton was published.

New York City became the leading theatrical city of the world.

The songs "Avalon," "I'll Be with You in Apple Blossom Time," "The Japanese Sandman" and "Look for the Silver Lining" were published.

The 1920s are known as the "flapper" age in reference to the irreverent attitude and stylish dress of the young women of the period.

The motorcar helped to promote the "roaring twenties."

The term "smoke-filled room" came into usage to describe political conventions.

Cleveland defeated Brooklyn in the World Series.

1921

politics

Warren G. Harding was inaugurated as the twenty-ninth president. Calvin Coolidge was his vice-president.

The first restrictive immigration act passed, allowing 357,000 immigrants per year.

General William Mitchell demonstrated the superiority of air power over sea power. His conclusion was not generally believed until later events proved the necessity of a national air force. Mitchell was posthumously promoted for his early recognition of this fact.

The U.S. and Germany signed a treaty of peace.

A telephone cable was laid to Cuba.

President Harding proclaimed Armistice Day a legal holiday.

The president dedicated the Tomb of the Unknown Soldier.

The Comptroller General of the U.S. was created by the Budget and Accounting Act.

The Teapot Dome oil scandal occurred over naval oil reserves in Alaska.

Congress passed the Federal Highway Act to provide for improvement of the nation's highways.

American farmers owned about 70 million cattle at this time.

There were 14.4 million acres of irrigated land in the U.S. this year.

Birmingham, AL became known as the Pittsburgh of the South.

The Disabled American Veterans organization was formed.

William H. Taft was named Chief Justice of the Supreme Court.

science & technology

Albert Einstein, a recent immigrant to the U.S., theorized that time is the fourth dimension.

arts & culture

Eugene O'Neill wrote *Anna Christie*.

Sherwood Anderson's *The Triumph of the Egg* was published.

The songs "Ain't We Got Fun," "April Showers," "I'm Nobody's Baby," "Ma, He's Making Eyes at Me" and "Some Day I'll Find You" were published.

Margaret Sanger helped to found the American Birth Control League in New York City.

WJZ of Newark, NJ broadcast the first play-by-play of the World Series.

The Miss America Pageant began.

Knee-length skirts came into fashion for ladies.

Dempsey knocked out Carpentier in the fourth round of the first prize fight to be broadcast on the radio.

1922

politics

Senator Kendrick of Wyoming introduced the first resolution that led to the Teapot Dome scandal.

The Federal Narcotics Board was created.

Mrs. W.H. Felton of Georgia became the first woman in the U.S. Senate.

The Lincoln Memorial was dedicated in Washington, DC.

President Harding was the first president to give a speech on the radio.

Pearl Harbor in Hawaii became a vital fueling station for U.S. Navy ships.

Congress passed the Cable Act which stated that women would no longer lose their citizenship if they married aliens.

The first German ambassador to the U.S. since the war, arrived.

science & technology

Dr. Alexis Carrel announced the discovery of white corpuscles in blood.

The first mechanical switchboard was installed in New York City.

The first fruitful research into radar in America was begun by the Navy.

Construction began on the Holland Tunnel between New York and Jersey City.

Vitamin E was identified in Berkeley, CA.

B.A. Fiske patented the first microfilm machine.

religion

Episcopal bishops voted to eliminate the word "obey" from the marriage ceremony.

arts & culture

T.S. Eliot wrote *The Wasteland*.

Tales of the Jazz Age and *The Beautiful and the Damned* by F. Scott Fitzgerald were published.

Babbitt by Sinclair Lewis was published.

Booth Tarkington wrote *Alice Adams*.

The songs "Way Down Yonder in New Orleans," "Toot, Toot, Tootsie," "Somebody Stole My Gal" and "Three O'Clock in the Morning" were published.

The play *Abie's Irish Rose* opened in New York.

Louis Armstrong joined a jazz band in Chicago.

In this year, 14,261,948,813 postage stamps were used by Americans.

Walker Cup golf matches were established in New York.

New York's National League team defeated New York's American League team in the World Series.

George Herman (Babe) Ruth became known as the "Sultan of Swat."

By now there were 30 radio stations and 60,000 radio sets in the U.S.

1923

politics

President Harding died at the age of 58 in San Francisco on his return from a trip to Alaska.

Calvin Coolidge was sworn in as the thirtieth president. The swearing in took place in Plymouth, VT and was done by his father, who was a justice of the peace.

U.S. troops were withdrawn from Germany.

Nevada and Montana enacted the first old age pensions in the U.S.

Oklahoma was placed under martial law by Governor Walton because of Ku Klux Klan activity.

President Coolidge delivered the first official presidential message on the radio.

The U.S. Senate held its first meeting on the Teapot Dome scandal.

science & technology

The Du Pont Corporation began production of cellophane.

U.S. auto production surpassed 4 million per year. More cars were manufactured in this year than in all 15 years of the industry.

The electric shaver was patented.

Vladimir Zworykin applied for the first patent on a television tube.

The first electric neon sign was installed in New York City.

The first chinchilla farm was established in Los Angeles, CA.

"Rubber paving" was tried but was not successful.

The sound motion picture process was unveiled in New York City.

The first auto balloon tires were produced on a regular basis in Akron, OH.

The railway from Seward to Fairbanks, AK was completed.

The first airplane smoke screen was demonstrated at Cape Hatteras, NC.

arts & culture

A Lost Lady by Willa Cather was published.

George Gershwin composed "Rhapsody in Blue."

The songs "Tea for Two," "I Want to be Happy," "Sonny Boy" and "Yes, We Have No Bananas" were published.

The "Charleston," a fast fox-trot, was introduced by ballroom dancers.

New York's American League team defeated New York's National League team in the first World Series to gross $1 million.

The first dance marathon was held in New York.

The weekly news magazine *Time* was founded in New York.

1924

politics

science & technology

arts & culture

Congress passed the Soldiers' Bonus Bill.

The Border Patrol was established.

Jimmy Carter was born in Plains, GA.

The Florida land boom was at its height.

The FBI was reorganized and J. Edgar Hoover was made its director.

The first women governors in the U.S. were elected: Nellie T. Ross of Wyoming and Miriam "Ma" Ferguson of Texas.

Montana Senator Walsh exposed the Teapot Dom scandal in Washington, DC.

Woodrow Wilson died at the age of 68 in Washington, DC.

Nevada was the first state to use lethal gas in executions.

New cars hit a low price of $290.00.

The Ford Motor Co. manufactured its 10 millionth auto.

A U.S. Army pursuit plane "raced the sun" from New York to California, gaining an hour in each time zone across the U.S.

The first contact lenses were imported.

The Black Canyon Dam was completed in Idaho.

The ice-cream cone machine was patented.

The chromium plating process was invented.

Eugene O'Neill wrote *All God's Chillun Got Wings* and *Desire under the Elms*.

Paul Whiteman's orchestra introduced symphonic jazz. In its first performance of "Rhapsody in Blue," composer George Gershwin was the piano soloist.

The operetta *The Student Prince* was produced in New York City.

The songs "Rose Marie," "Sweet Georgia Brown," "Indian Love Call," "Lady, Be Good," "I'll See You in My Dreams," "Yes, Sir, That's My Baby" and "The Man I Love" were published.

It was estimated that there were 2.5 million radios in U.S. homes.

Washington defeated New York in the World Series.

Trinity College in Durham, NC changed its name to Duke University, after tobacco millionaire J.B. Duke endowed it with a $40 million trust fund.

1925

politics

President Coolidge was inaugurated for his second term. Charles G. Dawes was his vice president.

The famous Scopes Trial opened in Tennessee, concerning the theory of evolution.

General Billy Mitchell was court-martialed.

Congress passed the Kelly Bill, encouraging aviation and airmail.

The U.S. Patent Office was transferred to the Commerce Department.

James J. Walker was elected mayor of New York City.

The Florida legislature passed a law requiring daily Bible reading in all public schools.

The national headquarters building of the American Legion was dedicated in Indianapolis, IN.

U.S. Marines were withdrawn from Nicaragua.

science & technology

The Du Pont Corporation began producing industrial alcohol.

Ronald Amundsen made the first attempt to reach the North Pole by plane.

An antitoxin for scarlet fever was prepared in Chicago.

The first dry ice was manufactured in Long Island, NY.

Relays of dog teams reached Nome, AK with an antidiptheria serum to combat a serious epidemic there.

The first potato chips were manufactured in Albany, NY.

The cosmic ray was discovered.

arts & culture

Willa Cather's *The Professor's House* was published.

Theodore Dreiser wrote *An American Tragedy*.

F. Scott Fitzgerald's *The Great Gatsby* was published.

The New Yorker was founded.

The songs "Moonlight and Roses," "Dinah," "Alabamy Bound" and "Always" were published.

The national spelling bee was begun by a Louisville, KY newspaper.

The new vogue for crossword puzzles reached its peak.

Pittsburgh defeated Washington in the World Series.

Tornadoes swept across dozens of towns in the Midwest, taking about 800 lives.

The movie dog Rin-Tin-Tin made the police dog a household pet in the U.S.

Fashionable ladies wore straight dresses with no waistline, and skirts above the knees.

1926

politics

Congress created the Army Air Corps.

The Distinguished Flying Cross was created by Congress.

The U.S. sent a representative to the disarmament conference in Geneva.

Congress passed the Civil Aviation Act for mapping airways.

A 26-year-old named Juan Trippe flew the first airmail from New York to Boston.

Boeing & Hubbard won the airmail contract between Chicago and San Francisco in the new "Boeing 40."

science & technology

The nation's first regular air passenger service was begun between Detroit and Grand Rapids, MI.

Henry Ford introduced the 8-hour workday and the 5-day workweek.

R.H. Goddard launched the first nonmunitions rocket in the U.S.

Ford Trimotor planes were developed at about this time.

The first photographs taken underwater in natural color were shot at Tortugas, FL.

The National Broadcasting Company (NBC) was formed in New York.

The first household electric toaster was marketed.

arts & culture

William Faulkner wrote *Soldier's Pay*.

Ernest Hemingway's *The Sun Also Rises* was published.

Eugene O'Neill wrote *The Great God Brown*.

The first book-of-the-month club was established in New York City.

The songs "One Alone," "After I Say I'm Sorry," "Are You Lonesome Tonight" and "I'd Climb the Highest Mountain" were published.

A devastating hurricane swept across Florida and the Gulf states, causing 372 deaths and $80 million in damage.

New Yorker Gertrude Ederle, 19 years old, was the first woman to swim the English Channel.

Gene Tunney defeated Jack Dempsey for the world heavyweight crown.

St. Louis defeated New York in the World Series.

Stanford University had the national football championship team.

Speakeasy bars and restaurants dispensing liquor were prominent. By now, nearly 2,000 violators of the prohibition law had died of poison liquor.

1927

politics

The first drilling was done for the memorial at Mt. Rushmore, SD.

Congress established the Federal Radio Commission.

Pan American Airways began carrying mail between the U.S. and Cuba.

President Coolidge announced, "I do not choose to run for president in 1928."

The Department of Commerce issued its first pilot's license.

science & technology

The first solo nonstop flight from New York to Paris was made by Charles Lindbergh.

The Columbia Broadcasting System (CBS) was established.

J.D. and M.D. Rust invented the mechanical cotton picker.

The Holland Tunnel was opened between New York and Jersey City.

The first iron lung was installed at Bellevue Hospital in New York City.

The television was first successfully demonstrated in New York.

The first telephone service was established between New York and London.

Handset telephones were replacing wall sets.

The first "talkie" movie was made.

arts & culture

Willa Cather wrote *Death Comes for the Archbishop*.

Ernest Hemingway wrote *Men Without Women*, a collection of short stories.

A Connecticut Yankee was the first outstanding Broadway success by Rodgers and Hart.

Show Boat opened on Broadway in New York City.

The songs "Ol' Man River," "Can't Help Lovin' Dat Man," "Bill," "Girl of My Dreams," "Me and My Shadow" and "Side by Side" were published.

The city of New York used nearly 2,000 tons of confetti in its parade for Lindbergh.

There were now 733 radio stations and 7.3 million radio sets in the U.S.

New York defeated Pittsburgh in the World Series.

Babe Ruth set his record with a 60-home-run season.

The first Golden Gloves boxing matches were held in New York.

A flood in the lower Mississippi Valley left 675,000 homeless.

1928

politics

Airmail service was established between the Twin Cities and Winnipeg, Canada.

President Coolidge attended the sixth Pan American Conference in Havana, Cuba.

Governor Al Smith was the first Catholic to make a strong bid for the presidency.

The Republicans used the slogan, "A chicken in every pot," in their presidential campaign.

science & technology

The first colored motion pictures in the U.S. were exhibited by George Eastman.

The first animated electric sign in the U.S. was installed on a Times Square building in New York.

Within a year of Lindbergh's flight, airline routes had doubled in mileage.

Jacob Schick patented the electric dry shaver.

The *Graf Zeppelin* made its first commercial lighter-than-air flight to the U.S.

Amelia Earhart was the first woman to fly across the Atlantic.

Ship-to-shore telephone service was established with the *SS Leviathan*.

A violent hurricane swept across Florida, causing 2,000 deaths and $25 million worth of damage.

The St. Francis Dam north of Los Angeles burst, causing 450 deaths and destroying 700 homes.

arts & culture

Eugene O'Neill wrote *Strange Interlude* and *Lazarus Laughed*.

Carl Sandburg wrote *Good Morning America*.

George Gershwin's *An American in Paris* opened in New York.

Mickey Mouse became a star in the first cartoon from Walt Disney Productions.

The movie *Wings* won the first Academy Award.

The songs "When You're Smiling," "Stout-Hearted Men," "Makin' Whoopee," "I Can't Give You Anything But Love," "Button Up Your Overcoat" and "Marie" were published.

WGY in Schenectady, NY was the first station to broadcast scheduled TV programs.

The U.S. won top honors at the ninth Olympic Games in Holland.

New York defeated St. Louis in the World Series.

Ty Cobb became the first baseball player to score more than 4,000 hits.

1929

politics

Herbert Hoover was inaugurated as the thirty-first president. Charles Curtis was his vice president.

The stock market crashed on October 29, triggering the Great Depression.

The U.S. had 825 bank failures from 1914 to 1929.

Franklin D. Roosevelt was elected governor of New York.

The last Allied occupation troops were withdrawn from Germany.

science & technology

Rear Admiral Richard E. Byrd made the first flight over the South Pole.

Construction was begun on the Empire State Building.

Lieutenant James Doolittle made the first instrument ("blind") flight in New York.

The Ambassador Bridge opened between Detroit and Windsor, Ontario.

There were now 44 scheduled airlines with 30,000 miles of airmail routes.

Color television was demonstrated.

Automobile companies produced a record 3 million cars this year.

arts & culture

Cole Porter's first hit show, *Fifty Million Frenchmen*, opened.

Ernest Hemingway's *A Farewell to Arms* was published.

William Faulkner wrote *Sartoris* and *The Sound and the Fury*.

Thomas Wolfe wrote *Look Homeward, Angel*.

The songs "When It's Springtime in the Rockies," "Wedding Bells Are Breaking Up That Old Gang of Mine," "Am I Blue," "Star Dust" and "Tiptoe through the Tulips with Me" were published.

The Museum of Modern Art in New York was founded.

Broadway Melody won the Academy Award.

Amos 'n' Andy began their radio career.

Philadelphia defeated Chicago in the World Series.

Notre Dame won the national football championship, with Knute Rockne as their coach.

The term "kickback" came into use to refer to a worker giving back part of his pay to retain his job during the Depression.

Al "Scarface" Capone was sentenced to a year in prison for carrying a concealed weapon.

1930

politics

The population of the 48 states at this time was 122,775,046.

Congress created the Veterans' Administration.

More than 1,300 banks in the U.S. closed during the first months of the Depression.

The Coolidge Dam in Arizona was dedicated.

Illiteracy in America reached a new low of 4.3% of the population.

Unemployment caused the State Department to virtually prohibit immigration of laborers from abroad.

Montana was the only state to lose population from 1920 to 1930.

The state capitol building at Bismarck, ND was destroyed by fire.

The national debt at this time was $16,185,309,831.00.

science & technology

A survey showed that 1 out of every 4.9 Americans owned an auto.

Astronomers in Flagstaff, AZ identified the planet Pluto.

The East Texas Oil Field was discovered.

The first pinball game was manufactured.

The Detroit-to-Windsor automobile tunnel opened.

Dr. Karl Landsteiner won the Nobel Prize for his discovery of human blood types.

The experimental electric passenger train was installed by Thomas Edison.

Boulder Dam, later renamed Hoover Dam, was begun in Nevada.

religion

Three Lutheran groups formed the American Lutheran Church in Toledo, OH.

arts & culture

William Faulkner wrote *As I Lay Dying*.

T.S. Eliot's *Ash Wednesday* was published.

Dashiell Hammett wrote *The Maltese Falcon*.

All Quiet on the Western Front won the Academy Award.

Television was still experimental, but station WEEI broadcast daily.

The songs "Three Little Words," "Sleepy Lagoon" and "I Got Rhythm" were published.

Philadelphia defeated St. Louis in the World Series.

A fire in an Ohio prison killed 320.

1931

politics

"The Star-Spangled Banner" was officially adopted as the U.S. national anthem.

Unemployment was estimated at between 4 million and 5 million.

In the wake of the 1929 stock market crash, 2,300 banks closed, 800 in two months.

President Hoover proposed an international moratorium on war debts.

Gambling was made legal again in Nevada, and casinos opened all over the state.

Savings and loan associations began in a suburb of Philadelphia.

science & technology

Steel production this year was only 13.5 million tons (down from 56 million tons).

The Empire State Building opened in New York. With 102 floors, it was the world's tallest building.

Dr. Urey made significant discoveries in nuclear physics.

The first successful rocket glider flight was made in Atlantic City, NJ.

The coaxial cable was patented.

The first electric dry shavers were manufactured.

The first commercial production of synthetic rubber began in New Jersey.

Thomas Alva Edison died at the age of 84 in West Orange, NJ.

The first diesel tractor was manufactured.

religion

The Federated Council of Churches of Christ in America defended birth control.

arts & culture

William Faulkner wrote *Sanctuary*.

Eugene O'Neill's *Mourning Becomes Electra* was published.

The Good Earth by Pearl S. Buck became a phenomenal best-seller.

Cimarron won the Academy Award.

The songs "Dancing in the Dark," "Good Night Sweetheart," "All of Me," "I Love a Parade," "Lady of Spain" and "Love Letters in the Sand" were published.

St. Louis defeated Philadelphia in the World Series.

Walter Lippmann began his syndicated column.

Iowa, Nebraska and South Dakota were overrun by hordes of grasshoppers.

Knute Rockne, Notre Dame's noted football coach, was killed in a plane crash in Kansas.

1932

politics

Unemployment in the U.S. reached 13 million. The amount paid in wages was now 60% less than in 1929.

The Reconstruction Finance Corporation was created.

Federal troops, under General Douglas MacArthur, drove the "Bonus Army" of U.S. war veterans out of Washington, DC. The veterans had assembled to demonstrate on behalf of an adjusted compensation bill entitling veterans to cash bonuses according to their length of service.

The cornerstone was laid for the new Supreme Court Building in Washington, DC.

Wisconsin was the first state to pass an unemployment compensation law.

A federal gasoline tax was enacted.

The average farmer earned about $341.00 per year after expenses, compared to 1919, when he earned $847.00.

The U.S. and Canada signed a treaty to construct the St. Lawrence Seaway.

science & technology

The San Francisco-Oakland Bay bridge was begun.

E.H. Land devised the first polaroid glass.

The first success in atom-smashing was achieved by Cockcroft and Walton.

arts & culture

William Faulkner wrote *Light in August.*

Ernest Hemingway's *Death in the Afternoon* was published.

Dashiell Hammett wrote *The Thin Man.*

Bank Night was introduced in theaters across the country.

The movie *Grand Hotel* won the Academy Award.

The songs "Brother, Can You Spare a Dime," "April in Paris," "Forty-Second Street," "Night and Day" and "Play, Fiddle, Play" were published.

Charles A. Lindbergh, Jr., the son of the famous aviator, was kidnapped from his home in Hopewell, NJ. He was 20 months old.

The Olympic Games were held in Los Angeles. The U.S. won 11 of 23 events.

Max Schmeling lost the heavyweight boxing crown to Jack Sharkey.

New York defeated Chicago in the World Series.

Baseball player Lou Gehrig hit four consecutive home runs in one game.

Gangster Al Capone began serving a 10-year prison sentence for income tax evasion.

The first motion picture drive-in theater opened in Camden, NJ.

1933

politics

Franklin D. Roosevelt was inaugurated as the thirty-second president. John N. Garner was his vice president.

The term "New Deal" was introduced by President Roosevelt in reference to his proposals designed to combat the poor economic conditions.

Prohibition was repealed with the enactment of the Twenty-first Amendment.

President Roosevelt proclaimed a "national bank holiday" and gave his first radio "fireside chat" when he reopened banks.

The Civilian Conservation Corps was organized to create employment.

The Agricultural Adjustment Act was created.

The Civil Works Administration was established.

The National Industrial Recovery Act was

created. This led to the establishment of the National Recovery Administration and the Public Works Administration.

Congress established the National Labor Board.

The Tennessee Valley Act was passed, establishing the Tennessee Valley Authority.

The Banking Act of 1933 established the Federal Deposit Insurance Corporation (FDIC).

The Home Owners Loan Corporation and the Farm Credit Administration were set up.

The U.S. went off the gold standard.

The average life expectancy in the U.S. was now 59 years, up 10 years from 1900.

The first U.S. aircraft carrier was launched.

The World Economic Conference held in

London demonstrated U.S. influence on the world economy.

The U.S. extended recognition to the U.S.S.R.

Adolph Hitler came to power in Germany as Chancellor of the Third Reich.

Calvin Coolidge died at the age of 80.

science & technology

Wiley Post flew the first plane solo around the world.

Albert Einstein moved to the U.S. permanently from Germany.

arts & culture

Erskine Caldwell wrote *God's Little Acre.*

James Joyce's *Ulysses* was allowed into the U.S. by a court ruling.

Cavalcade won the Academy Award.

George Balanchine and Lincoln Kirstein founded the School of American Ballet.

Popular songs of the day included "Smoke Gets in Your Eyes," "Stormy Weather" and "Easter Parade."

New York defeated Washington in the World Series.

Carl Hubbell of the New York Giants pitched his 45th scoreless inning.

1934

politics

The Federal Housing Administration and the Securities Exchange Commission were created.

The Federal Radio Commission was changed to become the Federal Communications Commission.

Puerto Rico requested statehood.

The intellectuals who joined President Roosevelt's administration were dubbed the "brain trust."

Richard M. Nixon graduated from Whittier College in California.

President Roosevelt visited Puerto Rico, the Virgin Islands, Hawaii and Haiti.

The Federal Savings and Loan Insurance Corporation (FSLIC) was created.

The president devalued the dollar to 59.06¢.

The National Mediation Board was created.

Alcatraz Island became the site of a federal prison.

Navy seaplanes flew to Hawaii from California.

At this time, 16 million Americans were on relief.

German Chancellor Adolph Hitler became "Der Führer" upon the death of President von Hindenburg.

science & technology

The Mutual Broadcasting System was formed.

Streamlined trains with diesel engines began to appear.

The Association of American Railroads was established.

One million members of the United Textile Workers went on strike across the U.S.

The Du Pont Corp. developed nylon.

arts & culture

F. Scott Fitzgerald's *Tender Is the Night* was published.

Eugene O'Neill wrote *Days without End.*

It Happened One Night won the Academy Award.

Cole Porter's *Anything Goes* opened on Broadway.

The pipeless organ was patented.

The songs "Deep Purple," "Cocktails for Two," "Anything Goes," "Isle of Capri," "Be Still My Heart" and "Winter Wonderland" were published.

Shirley Temple became known as the "Dimpled Darling."

Gangster John Dillinger was shot in Chicago. Charles "Pretty Boy" Floyd was shot in Ohio. Bank robbers Bonnie and Clyde were shot in Louisiana.

St. Louis defeated Detroit in the World Series.

Max Baer won the world heavyweight boxing championship.

A drought plagued the Midwest.

Western states were hit with earthquakes.

1935

politics

The National Youth Administration was established as a division of the Federal Security Administration.

The U.S. Supreme Court invalidated the National Recovery Administration.

Harry S. Truman was elected to the U.S. Senate.

The Works Progress Administration (WPA) was dubbed by some as "We Piddle Around."

Lyndon Johnson was named director of the National Youth Administration of Texas.

Gerald R. Ford graduated from the University of Michigan.

The Motor Carrier Act created the Interstate Commerce Commission.

The Rural Electrification Administration was established.

Congress passed the Potato Act to control potato production.

The Soil Conservation Service was created as part of the Department of Agriculture.

Congress passed the Public Utility Act.

Congress passed the Social Security Act, creating the retirement benefits system.

Governor Huey P. Long of Louisiana was shot in Baton Rouge.

science & technology

NBC demonstrated the practical use of the Zworykin television tube.

John L. Lewis established The Congress of Industrial Organizations (CIO).

The first parking meter was installed in Oklahoma City.

arts & culture

John Steinbeck published *Tortilla Flat*.

T.S. Eliot wrote *Murder in the Cathedral*.

Mutiny on the Bounty won the Academy Award.

George Gershwin's opera *Porgy and Bess* opened in New York City.

The songs "You Are My Lucky Star," "Moon Over Miami," "Cheek to Cheek," and "Begin the Beguine" were published.

Humorist Will Rogers and aviator Wiley Post were killed in a plane crash in Point Barrow, AK.

Alcoholics Anonymous was founded.

Dust storms devastated the Midwest.

Detroit defeated Chicago in the World Series.

Jim Braddock won the world heavyweight crown from Max Baer.

Beer was first sold in cans.

1936

politics

Congress passed the Merchant Marine Act, creating the Maritime Commission to set policy and the Maritime Administration to manage the U.S. shipping industry.

President Roosevelt promoted the "Good Neighbor Policy" to maintain peace in the western hemisphere.

The U.S. annexed Jarvis, Baker and Howland Islands in the Pacific.

Congress passed the Capital Gains Tax Act. The act instituted a general tax on the increase in the amount for which an asset is sold over its original price, minus any depreciation.

The U.S. Department of Agriculture announced that 336 counties in the U.S. had been ruined by the Great Drought (1934-1936).

Social Security went into effect.

Italy's dictator Mussolini seized Ethiopia. Germany signed pacts with Italy and Japan.

science & technology

Boulder Dam (later renamed Hoover Dam) was completed on the Colorado River near Las Vegas.

General Motors cut off the heat in its plant to combat a sit-down strike.

The first aviation gasoline (100 octane) was produced in New Jersey.

Douglas Aircraft introduced the DC-3.

The SS *Queen Mary* and the dirigible *Hindenburg* both arrived in New York for the first time.

The Triborough Bridge connecting the Bronx, Queens and Manhattan was dedicated.

arts & culture

Life Magazine was founded in New York.

Margaret Mitchell's *Gone with the Wind* sold over a million copies in six months.

The Great Ziegfeld won the Academy Award.

The songs "Bye Bye, Baby," "Is It True What They Say about Dixie," "Shoe Shine Boy" and "Pennies From Heaven" were published.

The play *You Can't Take It with You* opened in New York.

Bruno Richard Hauptmann was put to death in New York for the kidnapping and murder of the Lindbergh baby.

The Union Pacific Railroad established Sun Valley, Idaho as a ski resort.

The candid camera craze hit the U.S.

1937

politics

President Roosevelt was inaugurated for his second term. John N. Garner was his vice president.

President Roosevelt's phrase, "Prosperity is just around the corner," became well known.

The U.S. gunboat *Panay* was sunk by the Japanese in Chinese waters.

Congress passed the Neutrality Act loosening the American commitment to neutrality on the eve of World War II.

Germany's pride, the *Hindenburg* dirigible, exploded in flames over New Jersey.

Lyndon Johnson was elected to the U.S. House of Representatives.

Richard M. Nixon graduated from Duke University Law School.

Oil was discovered in Marion County, IL.

science & technology

The Golden Gate Bridge was dedicated in San Francisco.

The Lincoln Tunnel was built in New York City.

Howard Hughes established a new airplane record flight time from Los Angeles to New York of 7 hours and 28 minutes.

The National Cancer Institute was founded.

Pan American Airways' "Clippers" were now making flights to Manila and Hong Kong.

The first blood bank opened in Chicago.

W.H. Carothers patented nylon.

arts & culture

Ernest Hemingway wrote *To Have and Have Not*.

The dance the "Big Apple" became popular.

The Life of Emile Zola won the Academy Award.

Benny Goodman, the King of Swing, opened at Paramount Theater in New York.

The songs "Blue Hawaii," "Whistle While You Work," "Where or When," "Thanks for the Memories" and "Harbor Lights" were published.

Aviators Amelia Earhart and Fred Noonan, on a flight around the world, were lost over the Pacific Ocean.

The Dust Bowl devastated parts of Texas, Oklahoma, Kansas, Colorado and New Mexico.

Joe Louis knocked out Jim Braddock for the world heavyweight boxing crown.

A natural gas explosion destroyed a school in New London, TX, killing 294.

1938

politics

Congress passed the Fair Labor Standards Act, an omnibus bill regulating hours of labor, wages and child labor.

The Civil Aeronautics Authority was established.

New York was the first state to require medical tests for marriage licenses.

Congress formed a committee to investigate un-American activities.

The U.S. annexed Canton and Enderbury Islands in the Pacific.

The Naval Expansion Act was passed to build a "two-ocean" navy.

science & technology

The March of Dimes was organized to raise funds to fight infantile paralysis.

William Green was elected president of the A.F.L. and John L. Lewis was elected C.I.O. president.

Howard Hughes and four assistants made an airplane flight around the world.

There were 32,000 deaths caused by automobile accidents for the year.

Self-propelled combines began to be used in grain harvest.

Commercial production of nylon toothbrushes began.

The International Bridge between Point Huron, MI and Point Edward, Ontario was dedicated.

Chlorophyll was discovered.

arts & culture

William Faulkner wrote *The Unvanquished*.

Thornton Wilder wrote the popular play *Our Town*.

You Can't Take It with You won the Academy Award.

The songs "You Go to My Head," "September Song," "My Heart Belongs to Daddy," "Love Walked In" and "Jeepers Creepers" were published.

The "Lambeth Walk" was a popular dance step at this time, and the Jitterbug was flourishing.

Douglas G. ("Wrong Way") Corrigan flew in the wrong direction on a trip from New York to California and landed in Dublin, Ireland without a permit or passport.

A tropical hurricane took 460 lives in New England.

New York defeated Chicago in the World Series.

Joe Louis knocked out Max Schmeling to retain the world heavyweight boxing crown.

1939

politics

science & technology

religion

arts & culture

politics	science & technology	religion	arts & culture
President Roosevelt sought reassurance from Hitler and Mussolini that they would not attack any more nations.	The atomic bomb was brought to the attention of President Roosevelt.	The Methodist Church was reunited after 109 years of division.	John Steinbeck's *The Grapes of Wrath* was published.
The sit-down strike was declared illegal by the Supreme Court.	FM, or frequency modulation, was invented in radio reception.		*Gone with the Wind* won the Academy Award.
All warring nations were ordered to keep their submarines out of U.S. waters.	The first nylon yarn was manufactured.		The songs "Three Little Fishies," "Over the Rainbow," "South of the Border," "Beer Barrel Polka" and "God Bless America" were published.
The Townsend Pension Plan was defeated by Congress.	Pan American Airways began its transatlantic Clipper service.		World's Fairs were held in San Francisco and New York City.
Congress passed the Hatch Act, prohibiting government employees to be involved in political activities.	R.C.A. demonstrated television at the New York World's Fair.		The National Baseball Hall of Fame was built in Cooperstown, NY.
Germany invaded Czechoslovakia and Poland.	The $18 million Bronx-Whitestone Bridge, spanning the East River, opened.		New York defeated Cincinnati in the World Series.
Russia invaded Finland.	The first electric racetrack starting gate was installed in Inglewood, CA.		
Germany and Russia signed a nonaggression pact.	Nylon stockings became available to consumers.		
England and France declared war on Germany.	The first air-conditioned automobile was shown.		
Germany began bombing British towns from the air.			

1940

politics

The population of the 48 states at this time was 131,669,275.

Life expectancy in the U.S. rose to 64 years.

The Air Defense Command was established to defend the U.S. against possible attack.

Congress passed the first peacetime Selective Service Act.

The first parachute troops were trained.

President Roosevelt warned the nation against "unpreparedness" in the case of war.

Congress passed the Smith Act, making it unlawful to advocate the overthrow of the U.S. government.

The Food and Drug Administration was transferred to the Federal Security Agency.

The Kings Canyon National Park was created in California.

The America First Committee was

organized to challenge President Roosevelt's policy of intervention in the war in Europe.

The German word *blitzkrieg* (meaning lightning war) became well known as a description of German military attacks.

Denmark, Norway and France were captured by Germany.

The national debt at this time was $42,967,531,038.00.

science & technology

The first successful helicopter flight in the U.S. was made by Igor Sikorsky.

The Lake Washington Floating Bridge opened in Seattle.

The Gulf, Mobile & Ohio Railroad was incorporated.

Color television was demonstrated over a CBS station in New York.

The 40-hour workweek went into effect under the 1938 Fair Labor Standards Act.

arts & culture

Ernest Hemingway wrote *For Whom the Bell Tolls.*

Eugene O'Neill wrote *Long Day's Journey into Night.*

Thomas Wolfe's *You Can't Go Home Again* was published posthumously.

Rebecca won the Academy Award.

The songs "All or Nothing," "The Breeze and I," "How High the Moon," "You Are My Sunshine," "When You Wish Upon a Star," "This Is My Country" and "San Antonio Rose" were published.

An estimated 30 million Americans owned home radios at this time.

Cincinnati defeated Detroit in the World Series.

1941

politics

President Roosevelt became the first president to be inaugurated for a third term. Henry A. Wallace was his vice president.

On December 7, the Japanese attacked the American naval base at Pearl Harbor.

The U.S. declared war on Japan, Germany and Italy.

Congress passed the Lend-Lease Act, giving the President the authority to lend or lease equipment to any nation "whose defense the President deems vital to the defense of the U.S."

President Roosevelt and England's Prime Minister Churchill formulated the Atlantic Charter, a restatement of the principles of worldwide peace established after World War I.

The F.D.R. Library was dedicated in Hyde Park, NY.

The Civil Air Patrol was organized.

U.S. Defense Savings Bonds and Stamps went on sale.

President Roosevelt moved Thanksgiving Day to the last Thursday in November.

Gerald R. Ford graduated from Yale University Law School.

All German, Italian and Japanese assets in the U.S. were frozen.

"Remember Pearl Harbor" became a U.S. war cry.

Germany invaded Russia.

The national debt at this time was $64.3 billion.

science & technology

The Ford Motor Co. signed the first contract with a labor union.

The Rainbow Bridge opened across the Niagara River.

The first Quonset hut was built.

Grand Coulee Dam in Washington was finished.

Penicillin was developed.

arts & culture

F. Scott Fitzgerald's *The Last Tycoon* was published posthumously.

How Green Was My Valley won the Academy Award.

The songs "The White Cliffs of Dover," "Tonight We Love," "Deep in the Heart of Texas," "Blues in the Night," "The Anniversary Waltz" and "Chattanooga Choo Choo" were published.

New York defeated Brooklyn in the World Series.

"Praise the Lord and pass the ammunition" became a famous phrase and later a song.

Ted Williams was the first baseball player to hit over .400.

1942

politics

Rent ceilings, rationing and wage and price controls went into effect.

Gas rationing coupons were issued.

General MacArthur left Bataan, and Japan occupied Manila. The infamous death march of U.S. and Philippine prisoners of war was made to Japanese prison camps.

Free mail privileges were granted to the armed forces.

The draft age was lowered to 18.

Women enlisted in the military as WACS (Women's Army Auxiliary Corps), WAVES (Women's Naval Reserve Corps), SPARS (Women's Coast Guard Reserve), and Lady Marines.

Battles were fought at Midway, Guadalcanal, New Guinea, Coral Sea and North Africa.

The Office of Production Management (OPM) banned the sales of new cars and trucks.

U.S. B-17s bombed Rouen, France and B-24s bombed Naples, Italy.

Major General Doolittle led a bomber group over Tokyo.

"Victory gardens" sprang up across the U.S.

Navy flier D.F. Mason radioed the famed message, "Sighted sub, sank same."

The Farragut Naval Training Station opened at Lake Pend Oreille, ID.

The Manhattan District was organized for production of the atomic bomb.

The Works Progress Administration (WPA) was terminated.

Captain Eddie Rickenbacker was rescued in the Pacific.

The Office of Civilian Defense was established.

science & technology

As shipbuilding surged, H.J. Kaiser launched a 10,500-ton Liberty ship in a record time of four days in Vancouver.

The first jet plane was tested in California.

arts & culture

T.S. Eliot wrote *Four Quartets*.

William Faulkner's *Go Down Moses* was published.

Thornton Wilder wrote *The Skin of Our Teeth*.

Mrs. Miniver won the Academy Award.

The songs "When the Lights Go On Again," "This Is the Army, Mr. Jones," "Serenade in Blue," "Paper Doll" and "One Dozen Roses" were published.

In the worst single fire in modern U.S. history, 487 died at the Coconut Grove in Boston, MA.

Girls who wore stylish short socks became known as "bobby-soxers".

St. Louis defeated New York in the World Series.

1943

politics

President Roosevelt met with other Allied leaders at Casablanca, Cairo and Iran.

Battles were fought in Tunisia, Bismarck Sea, North Africa, the Aleutian Islands, Sicily, Italy, Rabaul and the Gilbert Islands.

General Dwight D. Eisenhower was named supreme commander of the European forces.

Scrap iron, steel and paper were collected in salvage drives for the war effort.

German Field Marshal Erwin Rommel (the "Desert Fox") surrendered in North Africa. Over 275,000 Axis prisoners were taken.

Nearly 500 Allied planes bombed Rome.

Mussolini resigned and, subsequently, Italy surrendered.

Race riots broke out in Detroit.

President Roosevelt declared that all American warplanes must be on a 48-hour week.

The Pentagon, the world's largest office building, was completed at a cost of $64 million.

The Thomas Jefferson Memorial was dedicated in Washington, DC.

By now, the war was costing the U.S. $8 billion per month.

science & technology

Radar began to be used in the armed forces.

Chicago's first subway opened.

arts & culture

Casablanca won the Academy Award.

The plays *Dark Eyes, Oklahoma* and *Kiss and Tell* opened in New York.

The songs "You'll Never Know," "Sunday, Monday, or Always," "Pistol Packin' Mama," "Mairzy Doats" and "I'll Be Seeing You" were published.

The movies *For Whom the Bell Tolls, The Human Comedy, Stage Door Canteen* and *This Is the Army* were released.

Notre Dame won the national football championship.

New York defeated St. Louis in the World Series.

1944

politics

The Allied forces launched the Normandy Invasion on June 6, D day.

Berlin was attacked by 800 U.S. flying fortresses.

U.S. troops made landings at Anzio, Nettuno, the Roi Islands, New Guinea, Saipan, Guam, Leyte and other islands.

The Serviceman's Readjustment Act (the G.I. Bill of Rights) was enacted.

Congress passed the Veteran's Preference Act.

Forty-four nations met at Bretton Woods, NH and established the International Bank of Reconstruction and Development for war-torn nations.

President Roosevelt froze all Argentine gold assets held in the U.S. in retaliation for Argentina's aid to Germany.

The U.S., Great Britain, Russia and China met

at Dunbarton Oaks in Washington, DC, and drew up a tentative charter for a world organization (the U.N.).

U.S. B-29 bombers made massive air raids on Tokyo, Japan.

Generals Eisenhower, MacArthur, Arnold and Marshall earned the rank of 5-star general.

science & technology

A New York City hospital established the first eye bank.

Streptomycin, an antibiotic, was first manufactured.

The first jet-propelled fighter plane was flown.

arts & culture

Tennessee Williams wrote *The Glass Menagerie.*

Going My Way won the Academy Award.

The songs "Sentimental Journey," "Rum and Coca-Cola," "Magic Is the Moonlight," "I'll Walk Alone," "Long Ago and Far Away," "Jealous Heart" and "Spring Will Be a Little Late This Year" were published.

The "Sad Sack" and "Up Front with Mauldin" were popular features in U.S. service newspapers.

St. Louis' National League team defeated St. Louis' American League team in the World Series.

The Ringling Brothers, Barnum & Bailey Circus had the worst circus fire in history in Hartford, CT when 107 people died.

Horse racing was banned in the U.S. because of the war.

1945

politics

arts & culture

President Roosevelt was inaugurated for his fourth term. Harry S. Truman was his vice president.

U.S. forces invaded Luzon, Iwo Jima, Okinawa and the Philippines in the Pacific.

President Roosevelt met with allied officials at the Yalta Conference.

U.S. and British bombers made 40,000 sorties over German cities in four days.

President Roosevelt died at the age of 63 at Warm Springs, GA. Harry S. Truman was inaugurated as the thirty-third president upon Roosevelt's death.

Representatives of 50 nations met in San Francisco to draft the charter for the United Nations.

It was reported that Hitler killed himself on April 30.

U.S. forces stopped at the Elbe River to wait for the Russians.

The Potsdam Conference was the last meeting of the Allied chiefs of state during World War II.

The gross product of U.S. goods and services was $215 billion for the year.

Germany surrendered at General Eisenhower's headquarters in Reims.

Many U.S. servicemen began returning home on the point system.

The first atomic bomb was exploded in a test at Alamogordo, NM.

Atomic bombs were dropped on Hiroshima and Nagasaki, Japan.

Japan surrendered to General MacArthur and Admiral Nimitz in Tokyo Bay.

The United Nations Charter was ratified by the U.S. Senate.

Most rationing ended with the war.

General George Patton died in an auto accident in Germany.

General Marshall resigned and was sent on a mission to China by President Truman.

Between 1942 and 1945, U.S. imports were triple the exports.

The Lost Weekend won the Academy Award.

The songs "Till the End of Time," "On the Atchison, Topeka and the Santa Fe" and "If I Loved You" were published.

Detroit defeated Chicago in the World Series.

1946

politics

The Atomic Energy Commission was created.

U.N. headquarters were established at New York City with a gift of $8.5 million from J.D. Rockefeller, Jr.

Voters in Alaska voted in favor of statehood.

Wage and price controls ended except on rents, sugar and rice.

Only 800,000 immigrants were admitted into the U.S. between 1931 and 1945.

Admiral Richard E. Byrd landed with his expedition in Antarctica.

The U.S. extended $400 million in aid to Greece and Turkey.

Jimmy Carter graduated from the U.S. Naval Academy.

President Truman proclaimed the Philippines to be a separate and self-governing nation.

President Truman officially ended the "state of hostilities".

The U.S. tested an atomic bomb near the Bikini Atoll in the Pacific.

War crime trials began at Nuremberg, Germany.

Winston Churchill, speaking at Fulton, MO, first used the term "iron curtain", to describe the border between communist and democratic Europe.

In the post-war baby boom, the U.S. population increased by 3 million.

U.S. servicemen's war brides began arriving in the U.S.

The national debt in January of this year was $280 billion.

science & technology

The first "autobank" was created in Chicago.

Over 4.6 million workers were involved in strikes during the year.

The A.F.L. voted to readmit the United Mine Workers under John L. Lewis.

The first electronic computer was completed in Philadelphia.

arts & culture

Eugene O'Neill wrote *The Iceman Cometh.*

Arthur Miller wrote *All My Sons.*

The Best Years of Our Lives won the Academy Award.

The songs "The Gypsy," "Doin' What Comes Naturally," "I Got Sun in the Morning," "To Each His Own," and "Tenderly" were published.

St. Louis defeated Boston in the World Series.

Ranch-style homes became popular at about this time.

In Atlanta, GA 127 died in a hotel fire.

1947

politics

Congress passed the Taft-Hartley Act, thus banning "closed shop" rules, regulating strike procedures and forcing unions to publicize their financial statements.

The Voice of America began broadcasting to Soviet-dominated areas.

The U.S. Air Force was established as a separate service.

Secretary of State George C. Marshall proposed the Marshall Plan of economic assistance, designed to prevent the spread of Communism in Europe.

The Presidential Succession Act designated the Speaker of the House and president pro-tem of the Senate as next in succession after the vice president.

The new Department of Defense unified all the armed forces.

John F. Kennedy was elected to the U.S. Congress.

Richard M. Nixon was elected to the U.S. Congress.

The peacetime draft was ended.

Colleges enrolled over one million veterans under the G.I. Bill.

Boulder Dam was renamed the Hoover Dam in honor of Herbert Hoover.

science & technology

The instant camera was invented.

Television sets began to be sold in the U.S.

The first airplane achieved supersonic speed in California.

Diesel engine buses replaced streetcars in New York City.

The first lens to provide zoom effects was demonstrated in New York City.

Tubeless automobile tires were announced in Akron, OH.

A telescope lens 200 inches in diameter was completed.

arts & culture

Tennessee Williams wrote *A Streetcar Named Desire*.

Thirty-eight U.S. magazines reached circulations of over 1 million.

Gentleman's Agreement won the Academy Award.

The songs "How Are Things in Glocca Morra," "If This Isn't Love," "There, I've Said It Again," and "As Years Go By" were published.

Jackie Robinson became the first black player in major league baseball.

New York defeated Brooklyn in the World Series.

Drive-in movies were becoming popular at this time.

In women's fashion, hemlines reached nearly to the ankles.

1948

politics

President Truman called the Eightieth Congress the "worst in our history".

Workmen's compensation laws were passed in all 48 states.

President Truman dedicated Idlewild International Airport in New York City.

Bernard M. Baruch introduced the term "cold war", describing the chilly relations between the U.S. and the U.S.S.R.

The U.S.S.R. blockaded Berlin, and the U.S. began its famous airlift to supply the city.

The U.S. experienced an economic recession.

The Marshall Plan appropriated $12 billion for Europe.

Kansas established a system to license liquor sales.

Congress passed the Selective Service Act, reinstating the military draft.

science & technology

New York City's subway raised its fare from 5¢ to 10¢.

Aureomycin, an antibiotic, was produced in laboratories in New York.

The conquest of pernicious anemia was complete with the discovery of vitamin B-12.

The first sliding-scale wage contract was signed by General Motors.

The first U.S.-built electric locomotive with a gas turbine was tested at Erie, PA.

CBS Laboratories developed the first long-playing records.

arts & culture

Norman Mailer wrote *The Naked and the Dead*.

Hamlet, starring Lawrence Olivier, won the Academy Award.

The songs "Buttons and Bows," "Baby, It's Cold Outside," "Candy Kisses," "On a Slow Boat to China," and "Tennessee Waltz" were published.

Babe Ruth and Orville Wright both died.

There were now 2,079 radio stations and 76,991,000 radio sets in the U.S.

Cleveland defeated Boston in the World Series.

"Citation" was the race horse of the year, winning 25 of 27 races.

1949

politics

Harry S. Truman was inaugurated for a second term. Alben W. Barkley was his vice president.

Truman's inauguration parade and ceremonies were the first ever to be televised.

The permanent U.N. headquarters was dedicated in New York City.

The U.S.S.R. ended the Berlin blockade.

Lyndon B. Johnson was elected to the U.S. Senate.

Gerald R. Ford was elected to Congress.

Mrs. Georgia Neese Gray became the first woman treasurer of the U.S.

President Truman revealed that the U.S.S.R. had detonated an atomic bomb.

Congress designated June 14 as Flag Day.

The North Atlantic Treaty Organization (NATO) was founded in Washington, DC.

From July 1, 1945 to September 30, 1949 $24,802,000,000.00 in grants and credits went to foreign nations from the U.S.

science & technology

A U.S. Air Force plane made the first circumglobal nonstop flight, refueling four times in the air.

Cortisone was first used as a treatment for rheumatoid arthritis.

A nationwide steel strike idled 500,000 workers.

An Air Force jet bomber crossed the continent in a record 3 hours and 46 minutes.

The U.S. fired the first rocket to reach outer space from White Sands, NM.

A new deep-sea record was set at 4,500 feet.

The minimum wage increased from 40¢ to 70¢ an hour.

arts & culture

T.S. Eliot wrote *The Cocktail Party*.

Arthur Miller wrote the popular play *Death of a Salesman*.

All the King's Men won the Academy Award.

The songs "Mule Train," "Mona Lisa," "Jealous Heart," "Bali Ha'i" and "Younger than Springtime" were published.

New York defeated Brooklyn in the World Series.

Canasta became the latest rage in card games.

1950

politics

The population of the 48 states at this time was 150,697,361.

President Truman ordered the development of the hydrogen bomb.

On June 25, North Korea crossed the 38th parallel into South Korea.

U.S. troops were sent to South Korea to aid in its fight with North Korea.

A state of national emergency was declared by President Truman.

President Truman called 62,000 enlisted reserves to active duty.

Seoul, the capitol of South Korea, was recaptured by U.S. troops.

U.S. troops crossed the 38th parallel into North Korea and reached the Yalu River. They then retreated under heavy attack from Chinese troops.

By October, troops from 16 U.N. countries were represented in Korea. The U.S. and South Korea represented about 90% of U.N. troops.

Seoul and Inchon fell to the North Koreans.

Illiteracy in America reached a new low of 3.2% of the population.

Alger Hiss was found guilty of two counts of perjury. He was accused of transmitting government documents to Russia.

Senator Joe McCarthy charged that there was communist activity within the State Department.

Congress created the National Science Foundation.

Richard M. Nixon was elected to the Senate.

science & technology

The General Motors Corporation reported the largest income ever by a corporation, $656,434,232.

Automobile sales in the U.S. averaged more than five million per year.

Tranquilizers were first synthesized.

The first kidney transplant operation was performed.

arts & culture

All About Eve won the Academy Award.

The songs "Autumn Leaves," "Sam's Song" and "Harbor Lights" were published.

New York defeated Philadelphia in the World Series.

1951

politics

The U.N. formally accused China of aggression in Korea.

The battlefront was pushed northward into North Korea.

The U.S. armed forces numbered 2.9 million at this time.

General Eisenhower assumed command of the Supreme Headquarters of the Allied Powers in Europe.

President Truman relieved General Douglas MacArthur of all commands in Korea.

The U.S.S.R. proposed a cease-fire for Korea at the U.N.

The first Korean truce talks were held at Kaesong.

Congress passed the Mutual Security Act, authorizing $7,483,400,000 in foreign aid.

Oil was discovered near Tioga, ND.

The U.S. exploded an atomic bomb underground for the first time at Frenchman Flat, NV.

Congress adopted the Twenty-second Amendment, providing that no president can serve more than two terms.

Julius and Ethel Rosenberg were sentenced to death for espionage.

Eisenhower resigned as NATO (North Atlantic Treaty Organization) commander in Europe to run for president.

science & technology

A.T. & T. was the first corporation to have over 1 million stockholders.

The first U.S. commercial color telecast was transmitted in New York City.

The first transcontinental telecasts were made.

Coast-to-coast dial service, without the aid of an operator, began.

Electricity was first generated from atomic energy in Idaho.

arts & culture

J.D. Salinger wrote *Catcher in the Rye*.

Herman Wouk's *The Caine Mutiny.* was published.

William Faulkner wrote *Requiem for a Nun*.

The U.S. had 659 symphonic groups at this time.

Over 190 million recordings were sold in the U.S.

An American in Paris won the Academy Award.

The songs "Slowpoke," "Tell Me Why," "Too Young," "On Top of Old Smokey" and "Shrimp Boats" were published.

New York's American League team defeated New York's National League team in the World Series.

"Citation" was the first race horse to win $1 million.

1952

politics

Puerto Rico became the first commonwealth of the U.S.

The truce negotiations in Korea deadlocked.

President Truman seized steel mills to prevent a strike by 60,000 workers.

The Supreme Court declared the government's seizure of steel mills unconstitutional.

The G.I. Bill of Rights was extended to Korean veterans.

The U.S. detonated its first hydrogen bomb in a test in the Marshall Islands.

Iowa became the first state to produce a $1 billion corn crop.

The national political conventions were televised for the first time.

Richard M. Nixon made his famous "Checkers" speech concerning political contributions.

President-elect Eisenhower visited the Korean battlefield.

science & technology

Cinerama was demonstrated in New York.

The superliner SS *United States* set a record by crossing the Atlantic in 3 days, 10 hours, and 40 minutes.

The American Medical Association and NBC televised for the first time the caesarean birth of a baby.

The New York Central Railroad ran its last steam locomotive in passenger service.

arts & culture

Truman Capote wrote *The Grass Harp*.

Ernest Hemingway's *The Old Man and the Sea* was published.

John Steinbeck's *East of Eden* was published.

The Greatest Show on Earth won the Academy Award.

The songs "Your Cheatin' Heart," "You Belong to Me," "Wheel of Fortune," "Blue Tango," "Anywhere I Wander," " Kiss of Fire," "Takes Two to Tango" and "Glow-Worm" were published.

Michigan State University won the national football championship.

Rocky Marciano won his forty-third straight fight and won the heavyweight crown.

New York defeated Brooklyn in the World Series.

The U.S. won a majority of events at the Olympic Games in Helsinki.

1953

politics

Dwight D. Eisenhower was inaugurated as the thirty-fourth president. Richard M. Nixon was his vice president.

The Korean armistice was signed at Panmunjom.

U.S. casualties in Korea totaled 157,530.

The U.S. experienced an economic recession.

Senator Wayne Morris of Oregon made a record-length speech of 22 hours and 26 minutes.

Former president Harry S. Truman retired to Independence, MO.

President Eisenhower opened Garrison Dam in North Dakota.

Senator Joseph McCarthy's investigations of prominent Americans stirred the national interest and gave rise to the term "McCarthyism".

John F. Kennedy was elected to the U.S. Senate.

The U.S. Communist party was ordered to register with the Justice Department.

The gross national product for the year was $365 billion.

The Small Business Administration was created.

The first atomic artillery shell was fired in Nevada.

science & technology

Federal margin requirements (percentages of the total investment price) for stock purchases were reduced from 75% to 50%.

A strike by the photoengravers in New York caused six major newspapers to suspend publication.

The first helicopter passenger service was begun in New York.

arts & culture

Arthur Miller wrote *The Crucible*.

Saul Bellow's *The Adventures of Augie March* was published.

From Here to Eternity won the Academy Award.

The songs "Ebb Tide," "Vaya con Dios," "That Doggie in the Window," "Rags to Riches," "Oh My Papa," "I Love Paris" and "I Believe" were published.

The game Scrabble became popular in the U.S.

Americans witnessed the coronation of Queen Elizabeth II in Westminster Abbey, London, via television.

New York defeated Brooklyn in the World Series.

The New York Yankees became the first team to win five World Series in succession.

1954

politics

The first atomic-powered submarine, the *Nautilus*, was commissioned in Groton, CT.

The world's largest war vessel, the aircraft carrier *Forrestal,* was commissioned in Newport News, VA.

The Air Force Academy in Colorado Springs, CO was authorized.

The U.S. and Canada announced the construction of an early warning radar net.

Five U.S. congressmen were shot on the floor of the House. All five recovered.

The U.S. and Japan signed the Mutual Defense Agreement, providing for the gradual rearming of Japan.

The U.S. and Canada approved the St. Lawrence Seaway.

President Eisenhower proposed a highway modernization plan.

Senator Joe McCarthy's dispute with the Army was aired on national television.

Congress voted to censure Senator McCarthy.

The Communist Control Act outlawed the Communist party in the U.S.

The Southeast Asia Treaty Organization (SEATO) was formed at Manila in the Philippines.

Between May 1953 and September 1954, 3,002 federal workers were discharged as security risks.

President Eisenhower propounded the "domino theory" of Communist expansion, whereby nations neighboring a Communist country inevitably come under Communist control.

The Supreme Court ruled racial segregation in public schools as unconstitutional.

science & technology

The gas turbine auto was demonstrated.

Dr. Jonas Salk began inoculating children against polio.

arts & culture

Tennessee Williams wrote *Cat on a Hot Tin Roof.*

William Golding's *Lord of the Flies* was published.

The "Cuban Mambo" suddenly became the craze with ballroom dancers.

On The Waterfront won the Academy Award.

The songs "This Old House," "Sh-Boom," "Mister Sandman," "Papa Loves Mambo," "Shake, Rattle and Roll" and "Teach Me Tonight" were published.

Studies showed that 60% of male and 30% of female Americans smoked, and that 64% of Americans drank beer, wine or liquor.

Three out of five homes in the U.S. had TV sets.

Juvenile delinquency was becoming a major civic concern in the U.S.

New York defeated Cincinnati in the World Series.

1955

politics

President Eisenhower held the first televised presidential news conference.

The Air Force Academy began operations at Lowry A.F.B., CO.

The United Nations now had 76 member nations.

Illinois became the first state to enact legislation requiring auto seat belts.

The U.S. announced plans for the first earth-circling satellite.

At this time, The U.S. had 4,000 atomic bombs stockpiled; the U.S.S.R. had an estimated 1,000.

The U.S. Senate pledged to defend Formosa (Taiwan) and the Pescador Islands.

The U.S. authorized $216 million in financial aid to South Vietnam, Cambodia and Laos.

The USS *Saratoga*, the world's most powerful warship, was launched in Brooklyn.

President Eisenhower suffered a heart attack in Denver, CO on September 23, but was able to preside at a cabinet meeting on November 22.

The U.S. Interstate Commerce Commission was ordered to end racial segregation on all interstate buses and trains.

President Eisenhower signed an order ending U.S. occupation of West Germany, but troops remained on a contractual basis.

The Warsaw Pact, a twenty-year mutual defense treaty among Albania, Czechoslovakia, Bulgaria, Hungary, Poland, Rumania and East Germany, was signed.

science & technology

The federal minimum wage was increased from 75¢ to $1.00 per hour.

The A.F.L. and the C.I.O. formally merged.

U.S. private investments abroad were estimated at $26.6 billion.

The first speedboat exceeded 200 miles per hour.

religion

The Presbyterian Church approved the ordination of women ministers.

arts & culture

Herman Wouk wrote *Marjorie Morningstar.*

William Inge wrote *Bus Stop.*

Marty won the Academy Award.

The songs "Dim Dim the Lights," "The Yellow Rose of Texas," "Ain't That a Shame," "Love is a Many-Splendored Thing," "Melody of Love," "Rock Around the Clock" and "Love and Marriage" were popular.

Brooklyn defeated New York in the World Series.

Davy Crockett caps were very popular with children at this time.

1956

politics

science & technology

arts & culture

Alaska adopted a state constitution.

The U.S. Senate rejected a proposal to change the electoral system to a system of nationwide popular elections.

President Eisenhower was successfully operated on for intestinal obstruction, and ran for reelection.

The bus boycott in Montgomery, AL was considered the first skirmish in the movement for black civil rights and brought Martin Luther King, Jr. to national attention.

Construction began on the interstate highway system.

Congress authorized private atomic energy plants.

The last Union Army veteran of the Civil War died at the age of 109 in Duluth, MN.

The first gorilla born in captivity arrived at the Columbus, OH zoo.

Around the World in 80 Days won the Academy Award.

The songs "Heartbreak Hotel," "No, Not Much," "The Poor People of Paris," "Blue Suede Shoes," "Mack the Knife," "Hound Dog," "Hot Diggity," "Memories Are Made of This," "Long Tall Sally" and "Moonglow" were popular.

American actress Grace Kelly and Monaco's Prince Rainier III were married.

Two airplanes crashed over the Grand Canyon, killing 128 people.

The famous Wanamaker Building in New York City was destroyed by fire.

The New York Coliseum, built at a cost of $35 million, opened as the world's largest exhibition building.

The Ringling Brothers, Barnum & Bailey Circus performed its

last show under the bigtop canvas.

New York defeated Brooklyn in the World Series.

The New York Yankees' Don Larsen pitched the first no-hitter in a World Series game.

Floyd Patterson knocked out Archie Moore for the heavyweight boxing championship.

1957

politics

President Eisenhower was inaugurated for his second term. Richard M. Nixon was his vice president.

President Eisenhower proposed the Eisenhower Doctrine, proclaiming that U.S. military and economic power would be used to protect the Middle East against Communist aggression.

Senator Thurmond of South Carolina set a new record, holding the Senate floor for 24 hours and 18 minutes.

President Eisenhower sent troops to Central High School in Little Rock, AR to enforce racial integration.

The first U.S. nuclear power plant began operating in Shippingport, PA.

A grand jury in Seattle indicted Dave Beck, the president of the Teamsters' Union for harboring criminals and plundering union funds.

The Distant Early Warning (DEW) radar defense line was put into operation.

The U.S. and Canada established the North American Air Defense Command.

President Eisenhower signed the first civil rights bill in 87 years.

The population of the U.S. topped 170 million.

Senator Joseph McCarthy died.

The U.S.S.R. launched *Sputnik I*, the first earth satellite.

science & technology

Three Air Force Strato fortresses circled the globe in 45 hours and 19 minutes.

A new type of influenza spread from China to the U.S. and became known as the Asian flu.

The electric watch was introduced in Pennsylvania.

A tidal wave caused by hurricane "Audrey" left 531 dead in Louisiana and Texas.

arts & culture

Jack Kerouac wrote *On the Road*.

Eugene O'Neill's *Long Day's Journey into Night* was published.

The Bridge on the River Kwai won the Academy Award.

The songs "All Shook Up," "At the Hop," "Blueberry Hill," "Bye Bye Love," "Great Balls of Fire," "Jailhouse Rock," "Lucille," "Peggy Sue" and "Wake Up Little Susie" were released.

The National Education Association celebrated its 100th anniversary.

Milwaukee defeated New York in the World Series.

1958

politics

The first U.S. earth satellite, *Explorer I*, was launched from Cape Canaveral.

Former president Truman charged that President Eisenhower had "surrendered" Korea.

The Air Force Academy moved to its permanent site near Colorado Springs, CO.

Warren Air Force Base became the first I.C.B.M (Intercontinental Ballistic Missile) base in the world.

President Eisenhower sent U.S. Marines to Lebanon during an insurrection there.

The new regime in Venezuela imposed restrictions on U.S. oil companies.

Robert H.W. Welch, Jr. founded the John Birch Society, a radical rightist political association.

At this time, about 70% of the U.S. population was urban.

Governor Faubus of Arkansas closed four schools in Little Rock to avoid segregation.

Presidential assistant Sherman Adams resigned under pressure after it was revealed that he had accepted gifts and done illicit favors while in office.

The National Aeronautics and Space Administration (NASA) was founded.

Vice President Nixon was jeered and pelted with rocks and eggs on a visit to Latin America.

The U.S. Post Office increased the cost of letter postage from 3¢ to 4¢.

science & technology

The U.S. nuclear submarine *Nautilus* made the world's first transpolar voyage, beneath the Arctic ice pack.

The U.S. nuclear submarine *Seawolf* stayed submerged for 60 days, setting a new world record.

An international auto show was held in New York City.

arts & culture

Truman Capote wrote *Breakfast at Tiffany's*.

Leon Uris wrote *Exodus*.

Gigi won the Academy Award.

The songs "All I Have to Do Is Dream," "Chantilly Lace," "Johnny B. Goode," "Rockin' Robin," "Splish Splash," "Tears on My Pillow," "To Know Him Is to Love Him" and "Tom Dooley" were released.

Texas pianist Van Cliburn won honors in Moscow.

A Gallup poll reported that Mrs. Eleanor Roosevelt was the most admired woman in the U.S. at this time.

Louisiana State University won the national football championship.

New York defeated Milwaukee in the World Series.

The New York Giants moved to San Francisco, and the Brooklyn Dodgers moved to Los Angeles.

1959

politics

Alaska became the forty-ninth state.

Hawaii was admitted as the fiftieth state.

President Eisenhower and Queen Elizabeth of England formally dedicated the St. Lawrence Seaway.

NASA picked its first seven astronauts.

Soviet Premier Nikita Khrushchev visited the U.S.

Khrushchev and Vice President Nixon had the famous "Kitchen" debate during Nixon's visit to Russia.

From 1820 to 1959, 41.5 million persons immigrated to the U.S.; 34 million of these were from Europe.

The New York Stock Exchange announced that 12,490,000 people now owned U.S. stocks.

After six attempts, Oklahoma voters repealed the state liquor prohibition.

The U.S. Air Force Academy graduated its first class.

science & technology

By now, oil had been found and drilled in 31 states.

By now, there were nearly 70 million motor vehicles registered in the U.S.

religion

The National Council of Churches announced that 64% of the U.S. population were church members.

arts & culture

Saul Bellow wrote *Henderson the Rain King*.

Norman Mailer's *Advertisements for Myself* was published.

Ben Hur won the Academy Award.

Songs released this year included "Charlie Brown," "Love Potion Number Nine," "Poison Ivy," "16 Candles," "Tallahassee Lassie," "Teen Angel" and "There Goes My Baby."

The "Cha-Cha" was the most popular dance at this time.

Director Cecil B. DeMille and actress Ethel Barrymore both died.

West Yellowstone, MT suffered a series of earthquakes.

The "beatnik generation", young people considered to be of radical social persuasion and dress, had appeared on the American scene.

Ingemar Johansson of Sweden defeated Floyd Patterson for the heavyweight boxing crown.

Los Angeles defeated Chicago in the World Series.

1960

politics

The population of the U.S. at this time was 179,323,175.

The Post Office Department established the first automated post office in Rhode Island.

The first nuclear powered aircraft carrier, the *Enterprise*, was launched from Virginia.

The *George Washington* was the first submerged submarine to fire a Polaris missile.

President Eisenhower's trip to Japan was cancelled because of riots there.

The 50-star flag of the U.S. became official on July 4.

Soviet Premier Khrushchev visited the United Nations.

Most Americans paid about 25% of their earnings in federal, state and local taxes.

Four black students performed the first sit-in by demanding service at a lunch counter in Greensboro, NC.

Congress held hearings on the "payola" scandal in the broadcasting industry.

A U.S. U-2 high-altitude plane was downed over Russian territory.

From 1951 to 1960, 2,515,479 immigrants arrived in the U.S.

Presidential candidates John F. Kennedy and Richard M. Nixon held four televised debates.

science & technology

The U.S. submarine *Triton* circumnavigated the globe in 84 days.

The SS *Hope*, a privately financed floating hospital, began a yearlong voyage.

John L. Lewis resigned as president of the United Mine Workers.

U.S. Navy bathyscaphe *Trieste* descended to a record dive of 35,800 feet.

Chrysler decided to discontinue its "DeSoto" line of cars.

Tiros I, the first weather satellite, was launched to photograph cloud cover.

arts & culture

John Updike wrote *Rabbit Run*.

Harper Lee wrote *To Kill a Mockingbird*.

The Apartment won the Academy Award.

Songs released this year included "Cathy's Clown," "Only the Lonely," "Spanish Harlem," "This Magic Moment," "Wild One" and "You Talk Too Much."

Pittsburgh defeated New York in the World Series.

1961

politics

John F. Kennedy was inaugurated as the thirty-fifth president. Lyndon B. Johnson was his vice president.

Outgoing president Eisenhower's administration severed relations with Cuba.

President Kennedy asked Congress for $1.8 billion for space and other programs.

The F.C.C. (Federal Communications Commission) began an assault on TV violence.

The Bay of Pigs invasion of Cuba by Cuban exiles organized by President Kennedy was repulsed.

The western states had a population boom. California now had a population of 16 million.

Cuban leader Fidel Castro offered to trade 1,214 war prisoners for U.S. tractors.

President Kennedy initiated the Peace Corps to aid underdeveloped nations.

Alan B. Shepard, Jr. was the first American rocketed into space.

The Congress of Racial Equality (CORE) began "freedom rides" into the deep South.

The practice of hijacking airplanes to Cuba was begun by Cuban nationals and Castro sympathizers.

The national debt at this time was $289 billion.

science & technology

Hurricanes "Carla" and "Esther", said to be the most fierce of the century, hit Louisiana, Texas and the Atlantic coast.

arts & culture

J.D. Salinger wrote *Franny and Zooey*.

John Steinbeck wrote *The Winter of Our Discontent*.

Joseph Heller wrote *Catch-22*.

Henry Miller's *Tropic of Cancer* had its first legal U.S. publication. (It was published in France in 1934.)

West Side Story won the Academy Award.

Popular songs of the day were "Will You Love Me Tomorrow," "Hey, Look Me Over," "Exodus," "Moon River," "Raindrops," "I Fall to Pieces" and "Where the Boys Are."

President Kennedy called for Americans to participate in more exercise and promoted jogging.

A poll of 276 newspapers voted the *New York Times* the best daily in the U.S.

Floyd Patterson retained his heavyweight boxing crown by knocking out Tom McNeeley.

New York defeated Cincinnati in the World Series.

1962

politics

Lieutenant Colonel John Glenn, Jr. became the first U.S. astronaut to orbit the earth.

Cuba offered to free 1,179 prisoners from the 1961 invasion attempt in exchange for $62 million in ransom.

U-2 pilot Francis Powers, held in the Soviet Union since his plane went down over Russian territory in 1960, was exchanged for a Soviet spy.

U.S. marshals escorted black student J.H. Meredith onto the University of Mississippi campus.

Richard M. Nixon was defeated in his bid for governor of California.

The U.S. loaned $100 million to the United Nations to help meet its financial crisis.

President Kennedy said that U.S. troops in Vietnam were there on a training mission, that they were "not combat troops in the generally understood sense of the word."

Congress approved the Twenty-fourth Amendment, banning poll taxes in federal elections.

President Kennedy faced down Soviet Premier Khrushchev in the famed Cuban Missile Crisis.

science & technology

NASA launched *Telstar*, a communications satellite, for AT&T.

arts & culture

John Steinbeck published *Travels with Charley*.

William Faulkner wrote *The Reivers*.

Ken Kesey's *One Flew Over the Cuckoo's Nest* was published.

Lawrence of Arabia won the Academy Award.

Popular songs were "I Left My Heart in San Francisco," "A Taste of Honey," "Misty," "The Twist," "Peppermint Twist," "Twist and Shout," "Can't Help Falling in Love" and "Sealed with a Kiss."

Albums released this year included Chubby Checker's *Your Twist*

Party and Joan Baez's *Volume 2*.

Actress Marilyn Monroe died of a drug overdose at the age of 36.

President Kennedy's love of rocking chairs sparked a new popularity for the chairs.

Seattle, WA held the first World's Fair in the U.S. in 22 years.

The University of Southern California won the national football championship.

New York defeated San Francisco in the World Series.

Sonny Liston knocked out Floyd Patterson for the world heavyweight boxing crown.

Jim Beatty was the first American to run an indoor mile in less than four minutes.

A record cash haul of $1,551,277 was taken in a mail truck robbery in Massachusetts.

1963

politics

President Kennedy was assassinated while riding in a motorcade in Dallas, TX. He was the fourth president in U.S. history to be assassinated.

Exactly 90 minutes after President Kennedy was pronounced dead, Lyndon B. Johnson was sworn in as the thirty-sixth president at a Dallas, TX airport.

President Kennedy's accused assassin, Lee Harvey Oswald, was shot to death by Jack Ruby on national television.

President Kennedy was buried at Arlington National Cemetery with an unprecedented number of world leaders from 92 countries in attendance.

President Johnson appointed a committee headed by Chief Justice Earl Warren to investigate the assassination.

An estimated 200,000 civil rights demonstrators

participated in a "freedom march" in Washington, DC.

The Senate held televised hearings on organized crime in the U.S.

Medgar W. Evers, an NAACP (National Association for the Advancement of Colored People) official, was shot by a sniper in Mississippi.

The "hotline" between the U.S. and the U.S.S.R. was established to help avert war.

The Supreme Court ruled prayers in public schools unconstitutional.

The U.S. lost $26 million in a "chicken war" with the Common Market countries in Europe over its levies on U.S. poultry imports.

Congress passed a bill providing for "equal pay for equal work, regardless of sex".

U.S. postage was raised from 4¢ to 5¢.

South Vietnam's President Ngo Dinh Diem was killed in a coup by the armed forces.

science & technology

The U.S. extracted 2.6 billion barrels of petroleum during the year.

The federal minimum wage was raised from $1.25 to $1.40 per hour.

arts & culture

John Updike wrote *The Centaur*.

William Carlos Williams's *Pictures from Brueghel* was published.

Tom Jones won the Academy Award.

Popular songs were "Call Me Irresponsible," "Wives and Lovers," "Blue Velvet," "Surfin' U.S.A.," "He's So Fine," "Sugar Shack," "Return to Sender" and "Blowin' in the Wind."

Albums released included Peter, Paul and Mary's *Movin'*, Joan Baez's *In Concert* and Elvis Presley's *Pot Luck*.

Los Angeles defeated New York in the World Series.

1964

politics

President Johnson declared his "War on Poverty" in a speech to Congress.

California surpassed New York as the most populous state.

The U.S. State Department revealed that the U.S. Embassy in Moscow was "bugged".

Cuba cut off the water supply to the U.S. naval station at Guantanamo, Cuba.

The U.S. and Panama resumed relations after negotiations for a new treaty regarding Panamanian sovereignty in the Canal Zone were begun.

Congress passed the 1964 Civil Rights Act.

Race riots in northern cities caused several million dollars' worth of damages.

James R. Hoffa, president of the Teamsters' Union, received a thirteen-year jail sentence for tampering with a jury and for defrauding the Teamsters' Pension fund.

Civil rights leader Martin Luther King, Jr. was awarded the Nobel Peace Prize.

The U.S. Senate authorized President Johnson to make unlimited expansion in the war in Vietnam because of the North Vietnamese attack in the Gulf of Tonkin.

Herbert Hoover died at the age of 90.

Douglas MacArthur died at the age of 84.

science & technology

U.S. Surgeon General Terry reported that cigarette smoking is dangerous to one's health.

arts & culture

Saul Bellow wrote *Herzog*.

Arthur Miller's *After the Fall* was produced.

My Fair Lady won the Academy Award.

Popular songs of the day included "I Want to Hold Your Hand," "She Loves You," "Hello, Dolly," "Love Me Do," "Louie, Louie," "Please Please Me," "Rag Doll" and "Baby Love."

Albums released included Peter, Paul, and Mary's *Blowin' In The Wind* and the Beatles' *Meet the Beatles* and *Hard Day's Night*.

Fiddler on the Roof and *Hello, Dolly!* opened on Broadway.

An earthquake in Alaska killed 117 persons and caused tidal waves in Oregon and California.

St. Louis defeated New York in the World Series.

The Mets and the Giants played the longest game in baseball history, 23 innings.

The U.S. won 36 gold medals at the Olympic Games in Tokyo.

Comedians Harpo Marx and Gracie Allen and songwriter Cole Porter died.

1965

politics

Lyndon B. Johnson was inaugurated for his second term. Hubert Humphrey was his vice president.

U.S. troops in Vietnam increased from 20,000 to 190,000 during the year.

The U.S. Senate investigated former secretary to the Senate majority leader R.G. (Bobby) Baker's activities and found him "guilty of many gross improprieties".

U.S. astronauts made several space flights and space walks.

Cheating scandals were discovered at the Air Force Academy.

The U.S. Government owned 773 million acres of land, or one-third of the nation's area.

Congress passed extensive Medicare, voting rights, and antipoverty bills.

President Johnson urged tourists to "see the U.S.A.," in the hope that domestic spending would offset deficits.

A plot to dynamite the Statue of Liberty was foiled in New York City.

Dr. Martin Luther King, Jr. led a civil rights march from Selma to Montgomery, AL.

A riot broke out in the Watts area of Los Angeles, causing 35 deaths and $200 million in damages.

U.S. troops were sent to the Dominican Republic to protect American citizens there after the deposition of the American-backed junta.

President Johnson had gallbladder and kidney stone operations.

President Johnson outlined to Congress his program for a "Great Society". The program's ideals were to eradicate poverty and to provide education and peace for all Americans.

Sir Winston Churchill died at the age of 90.

science & technology

The *Early Bird*, the world's first commercial communications satellite, was launched.

U.S. airlines carried 85 million passengers and over 10 billion tons of freight.

religion

Pope Paul VI addressed the United Nations.

arts & culture

Norman Mailer wrote *An American Dream*.

The Sound of Music won the Academy Award.

Popular songs of the day included "Satisfaction," "Downtown," "Help!," "My Girl," "Stop in the Name of Love," "Come See About Me," "Mr. Tambourine Man" and "Ticket to Ride."

Albums released included Barbra Streisand's *People* and *Beatles '65*.

The northeast U.S. had a massive 16-hour power failure, with more than 800,000 people trapped in elevators and subways in New York City.

Los Angeles defeated Minnesota in the World Series.

1966

politics

Massachusetts Senator E.W. Brooke was the first black in the U.S. Senate in 85 years.

W.C. Weaver became the first black to serve in a president's cabinet.

U.S. participation in the war in Vietnam escalated, and U.S. bombing of North Vietnam increased.

Movie actor Ronald Reagan was elected governor of California.

Medicare for the aged was inaugurated.

The U.S. abolished its "national origins" system in admitting immigrants.

At this time, 300,000 Americans were fighting in Vietnam.

The Supreme Court ruled that police cannot interrogate a person until he or she has been informed of his or her rights.

An unmanned U.S. spacecraft, *Surveyor I*, made a landing on the moon and sent back pictures of the moon's surface.

science & technology

Dr. Debakey installed the first successful artificial heart pump.

California grape growers and New York City newspapers both faced strikes.

arts & culture

The Metropolitan Opera moved to the Lincoln Center in New York City for its eighty-fourth season.

A Man for All Seasons won the Academy Award.

Popular songs included "You Can't Hurry Love," "Cherish," "Last Train to Clarksville," "Monday Monday," "Sounds of Silence," "California Dreamin'," "My Love" and "The Shadow of Your Smile."

The Beatles released their album *Rubber Soul*.

Walt Disney died at the age of 65.

Actors Clifton Webb and Montgomery Clift and gossip columnist Hedda Hopper died.

Miniskirts and paper throwaway clothes were popular at this time.

A berserk sniper shot 45 persons from a tower on the campus of the University of Texas, killing 14.

Illegal drugs, especially LSD, came into wide use among the American counterculture.

Baltimore defeated Los Angeles in the World Series.

The Motion Picture Association of America adopted a new code to distinguish adult films from children's films.

The New York *Herald Tribune* ceased publication.

1967

politics

Adam Clayton Powell was denied a seat in the Ninetieth Congress on the grounds that he had misused campaign funds.

The military announced that in 1964 the U.S. had lost 500 planes.

The number of U.S. troops in South Vietnam reached 474,300.

Unprecedented race riots occurred in 100 U.S. cities.

J.R. Hoffa, Teamsters' Union president, began serving an eight-year prison sentence.

Demonstrators against and for U.S. involvement in Vietnam marched in New York City.

President Johnson and Soviet Premier Kosygin met in Glassboro, NJ.

President Johnson and Mexican President Ordaz met in El Paso, TX.

The U.S. population reached 200 million.

Robert G. (Bobby) Baker was sentenced for his crimes.

Three U.S. astronauts were killed in a flash fire at Cape Kennedy, FL.

Thurgood Marshall became the first black to be appointed to the Supreme Court.

science & technology

The 100 millionth telephone was installed in the U.S.

The U.S. coal production force was now 10% of what it was in 1919.

The U.S. tanker *Torray Canyon* broke apart in the English Channel.

arts & culture

Leon Uris wrote *Topaz.*

William Styron's *The Confessions of Nat Turner* was published.

In the Heat of the Night won the Academy Award.

Popular songs included "Light My Fire," "Windy," "Respect," "Ruby Tuesday," "Somebody to Love" and "All You Need Is Love."

The Beatles released *Sgt. Pepper's Lonely Hearts Club Band.*

Actors Spencer Tracy, Nelson Eddy and Jayne Mansfield died.

The Green Bay Packers defeated the Kansas City Chiefs in the Super Bowl.

St. Louis defeated Boston in the World Series.

1968

politics

The USS *Pueblo* and its 83-man crew were seized in the Sea of Japan by North Korea.

North Vietnam launched the massive Tet offensive. As a major turning point in the war, the offensive led to the decimation of 80% of Vietnam's religious and cultural center, and raised questions about the ability of the U.S. to win the war.

President Johnson announced that he would not seek reelection.

Civil rights leader Martin Luther King, Jr. was assassinated in Tennessee.

Riots broke out in over 100 cities as a result of King's assassination.

Strikes and turmoil plagued San Francisco State College and Columbia University.

The first direct commercial flights began between New York and Moscow.

James Earl Ray was arrested in London as King's assassin.

Senator Robert J. Kennedy, aged 42, was assassinated in Los Angeles.

Sirhan B. Sirhan was indicted as Kennedy's assassin.

Postage cost was raised to 6¢.

Delegates from Washington and Hanoi met in Paris for preliminary peace talks.

Chicago police and National Guard battled demonstrators at the Democratic National Convention in Chicago.

Astronauts Borman, Andres, and Lovell circled the moon ten times in *Apollo 8*.

Campus revolts occurred across the U.S. and around the world.

science & technology

Workers went on strike against the Bell Telephone System for the first time in its history.

Hell's Canyon Dam was completed in Idaho.

arts & culture

John Updike wrote *Couples*.

Tom Wolfe's *The Electric Kool-Aid Acid Test* was published.

Oliver won the Academy Award.

Popular songs included "Hey Jude," "The Dock of the Bay," "Mrs. Robinson," "Hello, I Love You," "Green Tambourine," "Love Child" and "Jumpin' Jack Flash."

Simon and Garfunkel released *Parsley, Sage, Rosemary and Thyme* and *Bookends* and the Beatles released *Magical Mystery Tour*.

The U.S. won 45 gold medals at the Olympic Games in Mexico.

Detroit defeated St. Louis in the World Series.

The Green Bay Packers defeated the Oakland Raiders in the Super Bowl.

Jackie Kennedy married Aristotle Onassis.

Violent crimes had increased 57% in the U.S. since 1960.

1969

politics

Richard M. Nixon was inaugurated as the thirty-seventh president. Spiro T. Agnew was his vice president.

Astronauts Neil Armstrong and Edwin "Buzz" Aldrin became the first men to walk on the moon.

Astronauts Conrad and Bean made a second trip to the moon later.

An armed U.S. Marine forced a TWA plane to fly from California to Rome.

The U.S. had nearly 550,000 troops in Vietnam on January 1.

The gross national product at this time was $932.3 billion.

The Smothers Brothers' television show was cancelled for political reasons.

Black Panther party leaders were killed in Chicago.

The U.S. announced the return of Okinawa to Japan by 1972.

The trial of the Chicago Seven, a group of political activists accused of rioting at the Chicago Democratic Convention in 1968, began.

Dwight D. Eisenhower died at the age of 78.

science & technology

The world's first heart transplant on a human was performed in Houston, TX.

The blowout of an oilwell in Santa Barbara, CA contaminated 40 miles of beaches.

The Department of Agriculture halted the use of the poisonous insecticide DDT.

A $50 million nuclear submarine, the *Guitarro*, sank at a dock in California.

arts & culture

Philip Roth wrote *Portnoy's Complaint*.

Kurt Vonnegut wrote *Slaughterhouse Five*.

Norman Mailer's *Armies of the Night* was published.

Midnight Cowboy won the Academy Award.

Popular songs included "Aquarius/Let the Sunshine In," "Honky Tonk Woman," "Everyday People," "Hair," "One," "In the Year 2525," "Get Back," "Suspicious Minds," "Proud Mary" and "Bad Moon Rising."

Albums released this year included *The Beatles (White Album)*, and Creedence Clearwater Revival's *Bayou Country*.

Actress Judy Garland died at the age of 47 in London of a drug overdose.

Over 400,000 people attended the Woodstock Music Festival in New York.

New York defeated Baltimore in the World Series.

The New York Jets defeated the Baltimore Colts in the Super Bowl.

The murder of Sharon Tate and five others in Los Angeles resulted in the arrest of Charles Manson and members of his criminal "family."

1970

politics

The population of the U.S. at this time was 203,235,298.

A "sick-out" by federal air traffic controllers delayed or cancelled 1,000 flights in the U.S.

President Nixon made a tour of Europe.

Four students were killed and several more were wounded by National Guardsmen during a demonstration at Kent State University in Ohio.

Federal troops were sent to New York City to handle mail during a postal workers' strike.

Anti-war demonstrators were bloodied by construction workers in New York City.

President Nixon sent Congress the first "State of the World" message.

The Student Strike Center reported that 448 U.S. universities and colleges were either on strike or closed.

The Senate rejected funding for supersonic transport (SST) development.

President Nixon began putting federal armed guards on U.S. overseas flights to prevent hijackings.

The Army accused 14 officers in the 1968 My Lai massacre in which U.S. troops gunned down at least 450 Vietnamese civilians in South Vietnam.

Arab commandos blew up three hijacked airliners in the Jordanian desert.

The Environmental Protection Agency was established.

Congress limited cigarette advertising.

California Judge Haley and three others were shot to death in a San Rafael courthouse.

science & technology

The New York Stock Exchange bounced from its lowest point since 1963 to the largest gain ever posted for a single day.

The Penn Central Transit Company was allowed to reorganize under bankruptcy laws.

The University of Wisconsin announced the first complete synthesis of a gene.

arts & culture

Saul Bellow's *Mr. Sammler's Planet* was published.

Ernest Hemingway's *Islands in the Stream* was published posthumously.

Patton won the Academy Award.

Popular songs included "Bridge Over Troubled Water," "Let It Be," "Ain't No Mountain High Enough," "Signed, Sealed, Delivered" and "American Woman."

Albums released this year included Simon and Garfunkel's *Bridge Over Troubled Water, Abbey Road* by the Beatles, and *Deja Vu* from Crosby, Stills, Nash and Young.

Baltimore defeated Cincinnati in the World Series.

The Kansas City Chiefs defeated the Minnesota Vikings in the Super Bowl.

1971

politics

The Post Office Department was superseded by the semigovernmental U.S. Postal Service.

The draft law expired.

The astronauts of *Apollo 14* and *Apollo 15* made trips to the moon.

Mainland China was admitted to the United Nations, and Taiwan was expelled.

A bomb exploded in the Senate wing of the U.S. Capitol Building.

The U.S. pingpong team established "pingpong diplomacy" with China.

After a 19-month occupation, U.S. marshals removed 15 Indians from Alcatraz Island.

A prison riot in Attica, NY caused 37 deaths.

The cost of posting a letter rose from 6¢ to 8¢.

Lieutenant Calley was court-martialed for the 1968 My Lai massacre.

U.S. Vietnam War veterans tossed combat medals at the Capitol Building in a Washington demonstration.

The Vietnam peace talks in Paris began their fourth year.

President Nixon announced an 8.5% devaluation of the U.S. dollar.

The *Mariner 9*, orbiting Mars, became the first man-made object to orbit another planet.

The *New York Times* and the *Washington Post* published the Pentagon Papers, a forty-seven volume study, including confidential information on U.S. involvement in the Vietnam War.

In Washington, DC 7,000 demonstrators were arrested for trying to close down the U.S. government.

The Twenty-sixth Amendment became law, lowering the voting age to 18.

science & technology

Amtrak took over most U.S. passenger trains.

arts & culture

John Updike wrote *Rabbit Redux*.

Herman Wouk's *The Winds of War* was published.

The French Connection won the Academy Award.

Popular songs of the day included "Joy to the World," "It's Too Late," "Just My Imagination," "My Sweet Lord," "Maggie May," "You've Got a Friend" and "Me and Bobby McGee."

Albums released included Janis Joplin's *Pearl*, *Sticky Fingers* from the Rolling Stones and *Tea for the Tillerman* by Cat Stevens.

Pittsburgh defeated Baltimore in the World Series.

The Baltimore Colts defeated the Dallas Cowboys in the Super Bowl.

Charles Manson and three of his followers were sentenced to death for the Tate-LaBianca murders.

Hijacker D. B. Cooper parachuted from a U.S. jetliner over Washington state carrying $200,000.00 in ransom.

1972

politics

President Nixon made an unprecedented eight-day visit to China.

President Nixon ordered NASA to begin work on the space shuttle.

Pat Nixon made an eight-day tour of western Africa.

The U.S. incurred a $2.047 billion trade deficit, the first since 1888.

President Nixon made the first official presidential visit to the U.S.S.R.

The U.S. and the U.S.S.R. signed agreements on space and health.

After his meetings with the Soviet premier, President Nixon made a television address to the Soviet people.

The U.S. and Canada signed an agreement to cleanse the Great Lakes of pollution.

Alabama governor George Wallace was wounded in an assassination attempt in Laurel, MD.

Five men were arrested for breaking into the Democratic National Committee's office in the Watergate Hotel in Washington, DC.

The U.S.S.R. made an agreement to purchase $750 million worth of U.S. grain.

Militant Indians staged a week-long occupation of the Bureau of Indian Affairs in Washington, DC.

Astronauts of *Apollo 16* and *Apollo 17* made trips to the moon.

Harry S. Truman died at the age of 88.

The last of U.S. ground troops left Vietnam.

The national debt rose to $450 billion.

science & technology

A 135-day West Coast longshoremen's strike ended.

arts & culture

The Godfather won the Academy Award.

Popular songs included "American Pie," "The First Time Ever I Saw Your Face," "Lean on Me," "Heart of Gold," "Family Affair" and "Horse With No Name."

The Rolling Stones released *Hot Rocks 1964-1971,* and Carol King released *Tapestry.*

"All in the Family" was the leading television show in the country this year.

Clifford and Edith Irving pleaded guilty of faking an "autobiography" of Howard Hughes.

The first players' strike in the history of baseball delayed the opening of the season.

Oakland defeated Cincinnati in the World Series.

The Dallas Cowboys defeated the Miami Dolphins in the Super Bowl.

Bobby Fischer became the first world chess champion from the U.S.

1973

politics

President Nixon was inaugurated for his second term. Spiro T. Agnew was his vice president.

C.M. Kelley became the new chief of the FBI.

The U.S. and North Vietnam signed a peace agreement in Paris.

Indians made a 70-day siege at Wounded Knee, SD.

Black September terrorists killed the U.S. ambassador to the Sudan in Khartoum.

The U.S. and Cuba signed an agreement to curb airline hijackings.

Five men pleaded guilty, and two were convicted, of the Democratic headquarters break-in.

The U.S. and North Vietnam made an agreement for U.S. reconstruction aid to Vietnam.

U.S. prisoners of war began returning in groups from Vietnam.

The U.S. announced a 10% devaluation of the dollar by raising the price of gold.

Skylab, the first U.S. orbiting space station, was damaged shortly after it was launched.

The attorney general and two presidential aides resigned because of the Watergate affair.

The U.S. and the U.S.S.R. signed an agreement on troop strength.

The Senate select committee began public hearings on Watergate.

The Senate committee on Watergate learned of the White House tapes.

Vice-President Agnew resigned because of charges of tax fraud. He was replaced by Gerald R. Ford of Michigan.

An extensive controversy broke out among the Watergate investigators over the White House tapes.

A mistrial was declared in the Pentagon Papers case.

The Cambodia bombings ceased.

President Nixon ordered gas stations to close on Sundays due to the oil embargo.

A one-year delay was granted to the auto industry in meeting emission control standards.

arts & culture

Kurt Vonnegut wrote *Breakfast of Champions*.

The Sting won the Academy Award.

Popular songs included "Crocodile Rock," "My Love," "Touch Me in the Morning," "Killing Me Softly with His Song," "Superstition" and "You Are the Sunshine of My Life."

Albums released this year included Carly Simon's *No Secrets* and Pink Floyd's *Dark Side of the Moon*.

The Miami Dolphins defeated the Washington Redskins in the Super Bowl.

1974

politics

Because of the Watergate affair, Richard M. Nixon became the first president in U.S. history to resign his office.

Vice President Gerald R. Ford became the thirty-eighth president. Ford was the first president who was not elected to office.

Nelson A. Rockefeller became vice president.

Gasoline shortages caused long lines at gas stations in many states.

The U.S. ambassador to Cyprus was killed during a demonstration in Nicosia.

Gold sales became legal in the U.S.

Busing of students to integrate the public schools caused violence in Boston.

The national guardsmen involved in the Kent State killings were acquitted of wrongdoing.

President Ford pardoned Nixon for all crimes against the U.S.

Diplomatic relations were restored between the U.S. and East Germany and the U.S. and Egypt.

President Ford offered amnesty to draft evaders on an individual basis.

Indictments were handed down against seven Watergate defendants.

University of California student Patricia Hearst was kidnapped by a radical group called the SLA.

The World Food Conference held meetings in Rome.

arts & culture

The Godfather, Part II won the Academy Award.

Popular songs included "The Way We Were," "Come and Get Your Love," "Show and Tell," "Sunshine on My Shoulders," "Rock On," "Annie's Song" and "Sundown."

Elton John released his album *Goodbye Yellow Brick Road*.

Oakland defeated Los Angeles in the World Series.

The Miami Dolphins defeated the Minnesota Vikings in the Super Bowl.

Hank Aaron topped Babe Ruth's record for lifetime home runs.

Mohammad Ali knocked out George Foreman to regain the world heavyweight boxing crown.

1975

politics

President Ford raised tariffs on oil imports.

The U.S. experienced a deep drop in the gross national product.

Unemployment hit a 33-year high in January; the jobless rate was now over 8%.

A judge upheld the government's ownership of the Nixon papers.

The Bicentennial celebration officially began on April 19 when Lexington and Concord, MA celebrated the 200th anniversary of the battles that began the Revolutionary War.

Former Teamster president Jimmy Hoffa disappeared from a Detroit suburb.

Two assassination attempts were made on President Ford's life within 17 days.

New York City avoided bond payment default and financial bankruptcy.

President Ford reshuffled his cabinet in the so-called "Sunday Massacre."

The word "detente," meaning "relaxation," was widely used at this time to describe less tense U.S.-U.S.S.R. relations.

The world watched on television as Russian and U.S. spaceships linked up on the *Apollo/Soyuz* space mission.

Japan's emperor and empress made their first visit to the U.S.

The cost of posting a letter rose from 10¢ to 13¢.

science & technology

The Rock Island Railroad was threatened with bankruptcy.

Airlines were offering "no-frills" fares.

The federal minimum wage was raised from $1.60 to $2.10.

arts & culture

One Flew Over the Cuckoo's Nest won the Academy Award.

A Chorus Line opened on Broadway.

Popular songs included "Fame," "Shining Star," "Philadelphia Freedom," "One of These Nights," "Black Water," "Why Can't We Be Friends" and "Best of My Love."

Cincinnati defeated Boston in the World Series.

The Pittsburgh Steelers defeated the Minnesota Vikings in the Super Bowl.

1976

politics

Former president Nixon and his wife visited China at the Chinese government's invitation.

Secret bribes by Lockheed Aircraft caused worldwide repercussions.

Millions watched on July 4 as an armada of 225 sailing ships from 31 nations sailed up the Hudson River in New York during the bicentennial celebration.

Bicentennial wagon trains, some of which had been traveling for a year, converged in Pennsylvania.

After 200 years, the Liberty Bell was moved from Philadelphia's Independence Hall to a nearby pavilion.

Sex scandals plagued Washington, DC.

Ronald Reagan lost a close race to Gerald Ford for the Republican nomination for the presidency.

science & technology

The U.S. landed *Viking I* on the planet Mars.

The federal minimum wage was raised from $2.10 to $2.30.

The mysterious "Legionnaires' disease" killed 29 people at a convention in Philadelphia.

The Anglo-French *Concorde*, a supersonic transport, made its first flights across the Atlantic.

Millions took "swine flu" shots, but the project was later abandoned.

arts & culture

Saul Bellow wrote *Humboldt's Gift*.

Trinity, by Leon Uris, was published.

Kurt Vonnegut wrote *Slapstick*.

Rocky won the Academy Award.

The songs "Tonight's the Night," "Silly Love Songs," "50 Ways to Leave Your Lover," "Sara Smile," "Get Closer" and "Bohemian Rhapsody" were popular.

Two of the world's richest men died: J. Paul Getty at the age of 83, and Howard Hughes at the age of 70.

Twenty-six children were kidnapped and buried in a truck trailer in California. They escaped from the entombed trailer.

Romanian gymnast Nadia Comaneci starred in the Olympic Games in Montreal, Canada.

The Pittsburgh Steelers defeated the Dallas

Cowboys in the Super Bowl.

Cincinnati defeated New York in the World Series.

1977

politics

James Earl Carter was inaugurated as the thirty-ninth president. Walter Mondale was his vice president.

President Carter, in his first executive order, granted a pardon to draft evaders.

Congress voted itself a pay raise.

President Carter rejected building B-1 bombers in favor of cruise missiles.

Bert Lance resigned as President Carter's budget director.

The U.S. and Panama signed a canal treaty, to be ratified by Congress.

Farmers staged "tractorcades" in U.S. cities and towns.

Investigations began into Korean influence-shopping in Congress.

Andrew Young, the U.S. ambassador to the United Nations, became well known for his controversial speeches.

science & technology

Home video games played on television screens began to be marketed.

arts & culture

Network won the Academy Award.

Popular songs of the day included "You Light Up My Life," "Evergreen," "Dancing Queen," "Margaritaville," "Hotel California," "Nobody Does It Better" and "Dreams."

Stevie Wonder released *Songs in the Key of Life*.

Bandleader Guy Lombardo, actress Joan Crawford, singer Elvis Presley and actor Bing Crosby died.

Buffalo, NY and surrounding areas were paralyzed by snowstorms.

The Oakland Raiders defeated the Minnesota Vikings in the Super Bowl.

Racehorse Seattle Slew took the triple crown, and teen-age jockey Steve Cauthen had a record $6 million winning season.

New York defeated Los Angeles in the World Series.

The West Coast suffered from a severe drought.

The TV miniseries "Roots" broke viewing records and sparked a national interest in genealogy.

Over 3 million viewed the "Treasures of Tutankhamen" (King Tut) as the exhibit toured the U.S.

George Willig used mountain gear to scale the World Trade Center building in New York.

A lightning storm shut down New York City's electric power supply for 25 hours.

1978

politics

The U.S. Congress ratified the Panama Canal Treaty, thus transferring to Panama control of the canal and providing for a joint U.S.-Panama administrating body.

President Carter, Egypt's President Sadat, and Israeli Prime Minister Begin met for 13 days at Camp David, MD to chart a framework for peace in the Middle East.

California's Proposition 13, a tax-cut measure, triggered a taxpayer revolt across the U.S.

The city of Cleveland, OH caused a great commotion when it defaulted on paying bank notes.

President Carter announced that the U.S. would establish relations with the People's Republic of China.

Former vice-president Hubert Humphrey died.

The cost of posting a letter rose from 13¢ to 15¢.

The federal minimum wage was raised from $2.30 to $2.65.

science & technology

Three Americans were the first to cross the Atlantic Ocean in a hot-air balloon.

Louise Joy Brown became the world's first "test-tube" (conceived outside the human body) baby in Bristol, England.

Coal mines were shut down for 16 weeks by 160,000 striking miners.

religion

More than 900 Americans committed suicide in Jim Jones' People's Temple in Guyana, South America.

arts & culture

Annie Hall won the Academy Award.

The songs "You Don't Bring Me Flowers," "Miss You," "Staying Alive," "Shadow Dancing," "Three Times a Lady," "MacArthur Park" and "You're the One That I Want" were released.

Americans read more than 32,000 new books and saw more than 200 new movies during 1978.

Actor Gene Tunney and artist Norman Rockwell died.

The Dallas Cowboys defeated the Denver Broncos in the Super Bowl.

Leon Spinks won the heavyweight boxing crown from Muhammad Ali in February, and Ali won it back in September.

Fire destroyed over 25,000 acres and more than 250 homes in the Los Angeles area.

Over $6 million was stolen from New York's J.F.K. Airport in the largest cash robbery in U.S. history.

1979

politics

A malfunction occurred at the Three Mile Island nuclear plant in Pennsylvania, causing widespread concern about the safety of nuclear plants in the U.S.

America's first space station, *Skylab*, which was launched in 1973, landed in the Indian Ocean and Australia.

President Carter met with Soviet Premier Brezhnev in Vienna on SALT II.

President Carter met in Tokyo with six other national leaders on energy.

President Carter revealed plans for the U.S. to use the MX missile.

The price of gold exceeded $400.00 per ounce on the world market for the first time.

Gasoline prices topped $1.00 per gallon for the first time in the U.S.

President Carter created a new

Department of Education.

The U.S. gave up control of the Panama Canal.

Fifty U.S. diplomats were held hostage in the U.S. embassy in Iran.

Chicago elected its first woman mayor.

science & technology

The federal minimum wage was raised from $2.65 to $2.90.

The world's worst oil spill, from a Mexican-owned drilling rig, spread across the Gulf of Mexico and hit the U.S. Gulf Coast.

The Chrysler Corporation sought government aid.

religion

Pope John Paul II visited the U.S.

arts & culture

Tom Wolfe's *The Right Stuff* was published.

The Deer Hunter won the Academy Award.

Popular songs included "Bad Girls," "I Will Survive," "Le Freak," "My Life," "We Are Family," "No More Tears (Enough is Enough)" and "Chuck E's in Love."

In the worst airline disaster in U.S. history, 275 people died when a DC10 crashed in Chicago.

Forest fires blackened 400,000 acres of wilderness in eight western states.

Diana Nyad was the first person to swim from the Bahamas to Florida.

The Pittsburgh Steelers defeated the Dallas Cowboys in the Super Bowl.

Pittsburgh defeated Baltimore in the World Series.

1980

politics

The population of the U.S. at this time was 226,504,825.

Registration of young men for the draft was reinstated.

Because of the Soviet invasion of Afghanistan, the U.S. boycotted the Olympic Games in Moscow.

A U.S. attempt to rescue the hostages held in Iran failed.

The Canadian embassy in Iran smuggled six U.S. diplomats out of the country.

President Carter announced sanctions against the Soviet Union because of the invasion of Afghanistan.

FBI investigations uncovered the Abscam and Milporn scandals.

The Iran-Iraq War caused great concern in the U.S.

Double-digit inflation and a 20% interest rate (the highest in U.S. history) fueled an economic recession.

The U.S. spacecraft *Voyager I* sent back pictures of Saturn.

The Moral Majority organization had an impact on the national political campaign.

President Carter's brother Billy's relations with Libya led to investigations.

Race riots in Miami, FL caused over $100 million in property damage.

More than 125,000 Cuban refugees arrived in the U.S. in all kinds of boats.

Thirty-nine inmates died in a New Mexico prison riot.

For the first time in history, the price of gold topped $800.00 per ounce, and silver cost over $30.00 per ounce.

science & technology

The federal minimum wage rose from $2.90 to $3.10 per hour.

arts & culture

Kramer vs. Kramer won the Academy Award.

Popular songs included "Call Me," "Another Brick in the Wall," "The Rose," "Upside Down," "Don't Fall in Love with a Dreamer," and "Emotional Rescue."

Pink Floyd released their album *The Wall*.

Musician John Lennon was murdered in New York City. He was 40 years old.

Comic Jimmy Durante, actress Mae West, director Alfred Hitchcock and actor Peter Sellers died.

The Pittsburgh Steelers defeated the Los Angeles Rams in the Super Bowl.

Philadelphia defeated Kansas City in the World Series.

1981

politics

Ronald W. Reagan was inaugurated as the fortieth president. George Bush was his vice president.

After 444 days, the 52 American hostages were released in Iran.

The cost of posting a letter rose from 15¢ to 18¢.

The U.S. Census revealed that over half of the U.S. population now lived west of the Mississippi River.

President Reagan and three others were wounded in an assassination attempt.

The 11,500 members of the Professional Air Traffic Controllers Organization went on strike. President Reagan refused to allow them to return to work, and the union was disbanded.

Sandra Day O'Connor became the first woman on the U.S. Supreme Court.

U.S. Brigadier General James Dozier was held hostage by members of Italy's Red Brigade.

The U.S. launched the world's first fully operational space shuttle, the *Columbia*.

A major economic and business recession occurred.

The gross national debt at this time was $997,854,525,000.00, or $4,329.48 per capita.

science & technology

The federal minimum wage was raised from $3.10 to $3.35 per hour.

The medfly infestation threatened California's $14 billion agricultural industry.

arts & culture

Ordinary People won the Academy Award.

Popular songs included "Bette Davis Eyes," "9 to 5," "Rapture," "The Tide Is High," "Starting Over" and "The Winner Takes It All."

John Lennon and Yoko Ono's *Double Fantasy* was released.

Actors William Holden and Robert Montgomery, actress Natalie Wood and boxer Joe Louis died.

The Oakland Raiders defeated the Philadelphia Eagles in the Super Bowl.

Los Angeles defeated New York in the World Series.

Two walkways collapsed at the Kansas City Hyatt Regency Hotel, leaving 113 dead and 186 injured.

A huge sinkhole that swallowed up trees, cars, and buildings was created when the earth opened up in the town of Winter Park, FL.

1982

politics

The nation was in a deep economic recession, but the economy began to rally at year's end.

A memorial for the 57,939 U.S. soldiers killed or missing from the Vietnam War was dedicated in Washington, DC.

John W. Hinckley, Jr. was found innocent by reason of insanity for the 1981 shooting of President Reagan and three others.

The U.S. crime rate dropped for the first time in four years.

The Equal Rights Amendment was defeated after being ratified by only 35 states.

The U.S. provided about $280 million in economic and military aid to the government of El Salvador.

science & technology

Dr. Barney Clark was the first human in history to have his defective heart replaced with an artificial one. The surgical team was headed by Dr. William DeVries.

arts & culture

Gandhi won the Academy Award for Best Picture.

Ben Kingsley in *Gandhi* and Meryl Streep in *Sophie's Choice* took the Academy's top acting awards.

Kim Carnes' rendition of Donna Weiss and Jackie DeShannon's "Bette Davis Eyes" won the Grammy awards for record of the year and song of the year.

John Lennon and Yoko Ono's *Double Fantasy* won a Grammy for album of the year.

Authors Ayn Rand and John Cheever, Princess Grace of Monaco, actors James Broderick, Jack Webb, Henry Fonda and John Belushi and actress Ingrid Bergman died.

An Air Florida Boeing 737 crashed into the Potomac River after takeoff, killing 78.

The longest and most expensive pro football strike in league history took place.

Seven Chicago residents died after taking cyanide-laced Tylenol capsules.

The St. Louis Cardinals defeated the Milwaukee Brewers in the World Series.

1983

politics

arts & culture

President Reagan named two women to his cabinet: Elizabeth Dole as Secretary of Transportation and Margaret Heckler as Secretary of Heath and Human Services.

Sally Ride became the first American woman in space.

The U.S. space shuttle *Challenger* carried Guion Bluford, the first black astronaut, into space.

James Watt, U.S. Secretary of State, left office after public outcry over a racist and sexist remark that he made.

A terrorist truck bomb blew apart Marine headquarters in Beirut, killing 241 U.S. Marines.

U.S. and Caribbean troops invaded Grenada and overthrew the Marxist government.

Artist Christo "wrapped" 11 Florida islands in 6 million square feet of pink plastic.

Michael Jackson's *Thriller* album sold 20 million copies.

Singer Boy George of Culture Club gained national attention with his unusual appearance.

Dr. Barney Clark, the first human recipient of a permanent artificial heart, died 112 days after receiving it.

Author Corrie Ten Boom, playwright Tennessee Williams, composer Ira Gershwin, actor David Niven and actress Gloria Swanson died.

The Washington Redskins defeated the Miami Dolphins in the Super Bowl.

Baltimore defeated Philadelphia in the World Series.

A Pan-Am Boeing 727 crashed after takeoff in Kenner, LA killing 153 people, including 8 on the ground.

The East Coast was paralyzed by a February blizzard that left 35 inches of show. Thousands of travelers were stranded and 11 people died.

Vanessa Williams became the first black woman to be named Miss America.

Hawaiian volcanic mountain Kilauea erupted.

New York City held a 100th birthday party for the Brooklyn Bridge.

1984

politics

Ronald Reagan was reelected in a landslide victory at the age of 73, making him the oldest president in U.S. history.

Seventy-nine banks failed, the highest number in a single year since 1938.

A controversial CIA manual listing techniques of political assassination and guerrilla warfare was distributed to Nicaraguan rebels.

A suicide truck bomb blasted the U.S. embassy in Beirut, Lebanon.

Representative Geraldine Ferraro, a Democrat, became the first female vice-presidential candidate to run on a major ticket.

President Reagan used his emergency powers to provide aid to El Salvador after Congress had recessed.

General William Westmoreland filed a $120 million libel suit against CBS.

The Soviet Union and other Soviet bloc nations boycotted the Summer Olympic Games held in Los Angeles.

President Reagan visited China on a "journey for peace."

Twenty-four instances of bombings and arson were directed against abortion and family planning clinics.

science & technology

Two-week-old "Baby Fae" became the first human to be implanted with the heart of a baboon. She died 21 days later.

More than 2,000 people died in Bhopal, India due to a lethal gas leak from a Union Carbide plant there.

T. Boone Pickens led an attempted takeover of the Phillips Petroleum Co.

The first baby resulting from a donated embryo was born to a previously infertile mother.

A Supreme Court ruling made it legal to use video cassette recorders to tape films and TV shows.

arts & culture

Terms of Endearment won five Academy Awards, including best picture and Shirley MacLaine's award as best actress.

Robert Duvall won the Academy Award as best actor for *Tender Mercies*.

The Los Angeles Raiders defeated the Washington Redskins in the Super Bowl.

Detroit defeated San Diego in the World Series.

1985

politics

Shiite Muslim extremists held hostages from a TWA airliner for 17 days and killed one American.

President Reagan ordered partial economic sanctions against South Africa due to apartheid, the government-enforced policy of racial segregation.

Palestinian hijackers seized the Italian cruise ship *Achille Lauro*, killing one American.

U.S. planes intercepted four of the *Achille Lauro* hijackers in mid-flight and forced them to land on Italian territory.

John Anthony Walker, a retired Navy officer, and his son and brother were arrested and charged with espionage.

The 17-hour "Live Aid" concert, broadcast on radio and television, raised some $70 million for the starving people of Africa.

The Farm Aid concert, held in Champaign, IL raised over $10 million for U.S. farmers.

We Are the World, recorded by a group of top recording artists calling themselves USA for Africa, became an instant hit; 90% of the proceeds went to African famine victims, with the balance going to aid the hungry in the U.S.

science & technology

Broadcaster Ted Turner attempted a hostile takeover of CBS.

TV writers went on strike for two weeks.

Proctor & Gamble announced it would phase out use of its emblem on products due to rumors that the emblem signified the company was in league with the devil.

arts & culture

Amadeus won eight Academy Awards, including best picture and F. Murray Abraham's award for best actor.

Sally Field won the Academy Award for best actress for her role in *Places in the Heart*.

Lionel Richie's album *Can't Slow Down* won the Grammy Award for album of the year.

Actor Rock Hudson's death from AIDS increased nationwide concern over the disease.

A record 115,930,000 watched as the San Francisco Forty-Niners defeated the Miami Dolphins in the Super Bowl.

Kansas City defeated St. Louis in the World Series.

1986

politics

*arts &
culture*

The Gramm-Rudman budget law was declared unconstitutional by the Supreme Court.

U.S. jets bombed "terrorist-related" Libyan targets in retaliation for the bombing of a West Berlin discotheque in which a U.S. serviceman was killed.

Congress worked on a well-publicized tax reform package.

Warren E. Burger resigned as chief justice of the United States after serving on the Supreme Court for 17 years.

The space shuttle *Challenger* exploded shortly after launching, killing all seven crew members, including Christa McAuliffe, the first "citizen observer" to ride the shuttle.

Workplace sexual harassment was held to be illegal by the Supreme Court.

Many Americans cancelled plans for

foreign travel due to a spate of terrorist attacks abroad aimed at Americans.

In "Hands Across America" more than 5 million Americans held hands in a human chain that stretched virtually across America to raise money for and public awareness of the homeless and poverty-stricken in America.

Poet, essayist and novelist Robert Penn Warren was named the first U.S. Poet Laureate.

Out of Africa won seven Academy Awards, including best picture.

William Hurt won the Academy Award for best actor for his role in *Kiss of the Spider Woman*.

Geraldine Page won the Academy Award for best actress for her role in *The Trip to Bountiful*.

The Chicago Bears defeated the New England Patriots in the Super Bowl.

Halley's comet was visible to the unaided eye off and on throughout the first part of the year.

A four-day celebration took place in New York City marking the Statue of Liberty's restoration, the statue's 100th anniversary, and the 210th anniversary of the U.S.

1987

politics

The 100th Congress convened with Democratic majorities in both the House and the Senate for the first time since President Reagan's election in 1980.

President Reagan submitted the nation's first trillion-dollar budget.

The government reported unemployment to be at the lowest level in six years.

The Dow Jones stock average topped the 2,000 mark.

10,000 civil rights supporters marched on the all-white town of Cumming, GA. The march was disrupted by Ku Klux Klan members.

Securities trader Dennis Levine, whose confession to stock fraud in 1986 had helped uncover a major insider trading scandal, was sentenced to two years in prison.

Michael K. Deaver, friend and key aide to President Reagan, was indicted on charges of perjury during an investigation of his possible involvement in illegal lobbying activities.

The House voted to suspend aid to the Nicaraguan Contras until President Reagan could explain the funding sent to the Contras during a period of congressional prohibition of government-funded aid.

Clayton Lonetree, Marine Corps embassy guard in Moscow, faced charges of espionage after his association with a female KGB agent was revealed.

Seventeen mobsters were convicted in the "Pizza Connection" organized crime trial.

science & technology

The first drug for the treatment of AIDS, AZT, was approved by the Food and Drug Administration.

The first human test of an AIDS vaccine was conducted.

A pair of German Siamese twins were successfully separated in a 22-hour operation performed by a 70-person medical team in a Baltimore hospital.

A moderately severe earthquake measuring 6.1 on the Richter scale struck Southern California on October 1st.

religion

TV evangelist Jim Bakker resigned his ministry after accusations of adultery and financial misconduct.

A Federal District Court ruling holding that public schools in Hawkins, TN could excuse students because textbooks offended their parents' religious beliefs was overturned.

arts & culture

Van Gogh's painting "Sunflowers" was auctioned for $39,900,000.00, the highest amount ever paid for a work of art at auction.

Richard Wilbur was named the second U.S. Poet Laureate.

Platoon won the Academy Award for Best Picture.

A 24-day professional football players' strike ended without achieving its objectives.

The Minnesota Twins won the World Series against the St. Louis Cardinals. This was the first Series which was played (partially) indoors.

The New York Giants beat the Denver Broncos in the Super Bowl.

Ivan Lendl and Martina Navratilova became the U.S. Open singles champions.

1988

politics

*science &
technology*

1988

religion

arts &
culture

1989

politics

science & technology

1989

religion

*arts &
culture*